GREEN BELT

MODERN LANDSCAPE DESIGN

PAGE ONE

GREEN BELT

Modern Landscape Design

CONTENTS

Parks

Allerpark Wolfsburg 008

Oschatz Park 016

Carlebach Park 022

BUGA Munich 2005 028

Diana Princess of Wales Memorial 034

State Horticultural Garden Show Eberswalde 040

IGA - International Garden Exhibition Rostock 046

Grosses Holz Spoil Heap 052

Garden of Knowledge 058

Wernigerode State Horticultural Show 2006 064

Squares

070   Marstall Square Munich – Stage for Urban Life

076   Plaza of the Human Rights

080   Georg-Freundorfer Plaza

086   Festival Hall of Weissach

092   Tessinerplatz

098   Heinz Raspe Plaza

contents

Commercial

104   Alcântara Rio

112   Trumpf-Sachsen

118   Living and Working in Park City

124   Federal Environmental Agency - Nature in Motion

130   Innovations Centre Getrag Company

136   Common Ground

142   Headquarter Infineon Campeon

148   Swiss Life

154   Innovation Center for Environment Technology

Residential

Casa Blanca 160

Spreekarree 166

Nicolaas Beetsplein 172

Residential Building Riem 178

Louis-Häfliger-Park 182

Old Print Factory 186

contents

Waterfronts

Tejo and Trancão Park 190

Schiffbauergasse (Ship Builder Lane) Potsdam 196

Spandau Havel Promenade 202

Limmatstufen im Wipkingerpark 208

Old / New Harbour Bremerhaven 212

Educational

216   University of Applied Sciences

222   MPSO Buttikon

228   Primaries School at the promenade of freedom

234   TU Munich-Garching

240   Surrounding School House Central Grüningen

contents

Private Gardens

246   Guesthouse Münchener Rück

250   Roof Garden

254   Privat Garten Dietikon

268   The Garden without the direction

FOREWORD

Green Belt: Modern Landscape Architecture shows the newest and most important work of landscape architects worldwide.

Landscape architecture today is characterised by manifold styles and impressions, united by the aim of finding new innovative solutions for our living environment. A 'green belt' is an expression for a landscape that is created by humans as a living environment. Green belts are located in the urban structure and run the gamut of forms and styles. This collection of landscape architecture aims to give the public access to the current state of creative landscape architecture, and is organised according to the different functions of the designs. Architects from all over the world, including Germany, Austria, the Netherlands, Switzerland, Japan and the United States have been invited to show their work in this volume.

With the aim of showing high quality creative landscape architecture rooted in conceptual aspects such as analogies to context, function, shapes and material, we hope this collection of works will come as a source of creativity and inspiration to architects all over the world.

M.A. Dipl.-Ing. Daniel Schulz

A entrance sightseen platform
B allerpark central area

Allerpark Wolfsburg

Landscape:	Büro Kiefer
Location:	Wolfsburg, Germany
Client:	Wolfsburg AG
Completion:	2004
Size:	130.000 m^2
Costs:	12.790.000 €
Photographs:	Hanns Joosten

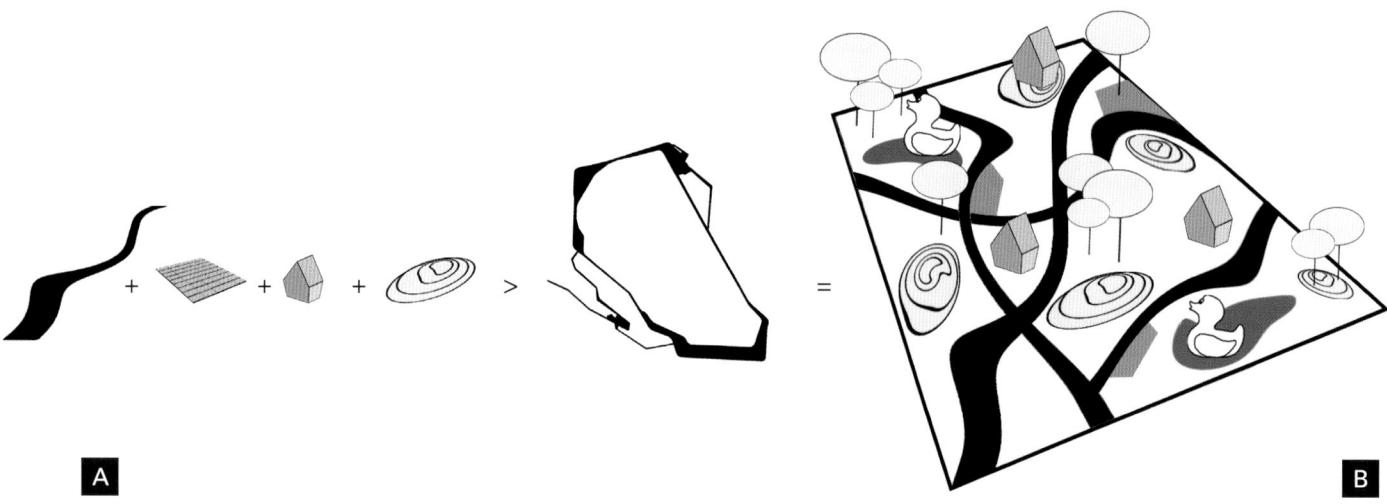

A   B

Office Kiefer created the prototype of the 'intermediate city' park with the 'Wolfsburg World of Adventure', created for the Land Horticultural Show in 2004. Visitors experience a park that makes them curious even from a distance because of its unusually staggered height. Hitherto, major elements of Wolfsburg were largely packed very close together north-east of the 'Middle Land Channel'. The brick buildings of the VW factory are the dominant feature. More recent additions are next to them. Extensive car park sports fields, the new VfL Wolfsburg football stadium and the Allersee, a former gravel pit, which has been upgraded as an intensively used local recreation area. The first element in the rearrangement of this area was the 'Autostadt' (Car City).This 'brandscape' with its artificial waterways, recreation areas, hotel and restaurants and presentation facilities for the VW world of brands now forms an extension of the VW site. The 'Autostadt' was planned by Henn Architekten with WES & Partner, and set international standards. The 'Allerpark World of Adventure' picks up where this left off.

The brief for the Allerpark was to present a whole variety of views and atmospheres in a confined space in terms of landscape architecture. At the same time, the new park was to address the city's leisure potential. Even in the first few meters the setting opens up more with every step after passing an austerely conceived steel edge. The landscape is framed in Corten steel, and staggered and folded upwards in a way that has never been seen hitherto, thus making a particular impact in this intermediate urban situation. It is this spatial quality, matched by the use of material (Corten steel, water, wood) that makes the new Allerpark into a self-confident piece of urban landscape. The Allerpark is intended for movement and dynamics, not for astonished staring. After the Horticultural Show it is to be used by skaters and downhill bikers, not just fans of water-skiing. And so when looking down from the new hills, the 'bastions', the eye is confronted with the prototype of an intermediate urban landscape. Büro Kiefer designed a park appropriate to this place. Mobility is active leisure, while the cars take a break. The traffic flows between much that is at rest. And above it all are the chimneys of the VW factory.

A concept scheme

B site plan

C corten steel elements

A

A sightseen platform

B corten steel elements

A

A lake scenery

B footpath through the park

A playground
B foot bridge from upper level

Oschatz Park

Landscape:	Weidinger Landscape Architects
Location:	Oschatz, Germany
Client:	City of Oschatz
Completion:	2006
Size:	15 ha
Costs:	9.000.000 €
Photographs:	Hanns Joosten

The city Oschatz decided to build a new linear park along the river, which links the historic city and the surrounding landscape. The city's wish was to integrate a little zoo and a pedagogical program about life of animals and about botanical and horticultural phenomena.

These programs were organized in hedged spaces. The height of the carpinus betulus hedges is 2.30 m, so that the promenade could' t overlook them. Entering the garden is a surprise. The promenade is like adventuring a palace.

In the gardens you find animals, particular plantings, like rose garden or garden of succulents, playgrounds, mini golf, water, vertical garden and a maze. The hedges cover the entire necessary infrastructure for the animals. The polygonal hedge structure reminds of baroque gardens, but the special perception is a very contemporary one.

A new building for winter playground marks the center of the park. The building on a circle ground plan is surrounded by a ramp, which leads up old town, which is situated 8 m above the park level. The lake as the final element of the park has two different lakeshores, a cultivated one next to the park and a natural one going out in the landscape.

B

C

A master plan

B islands of flowers

C playground - labyrinth

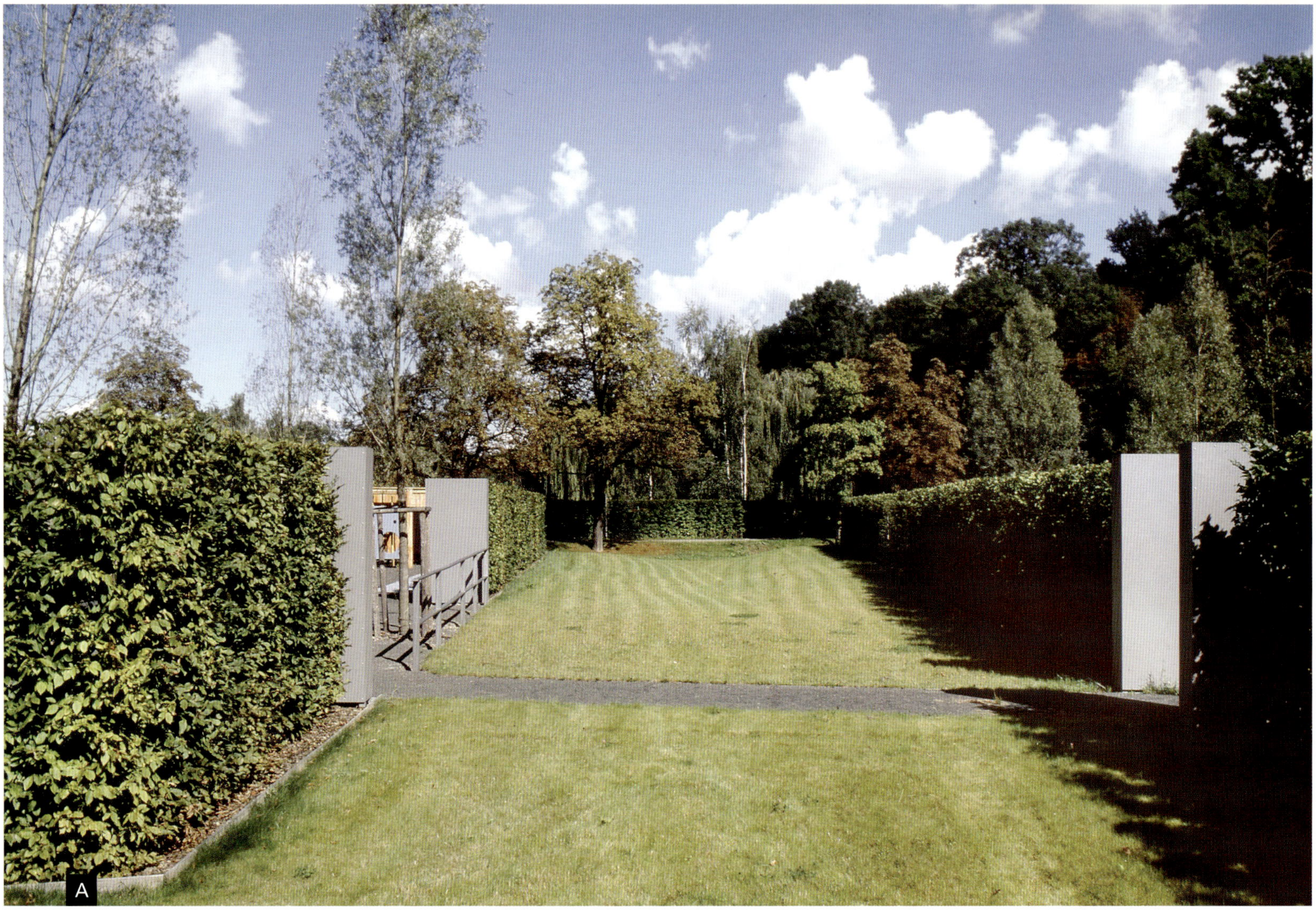

A

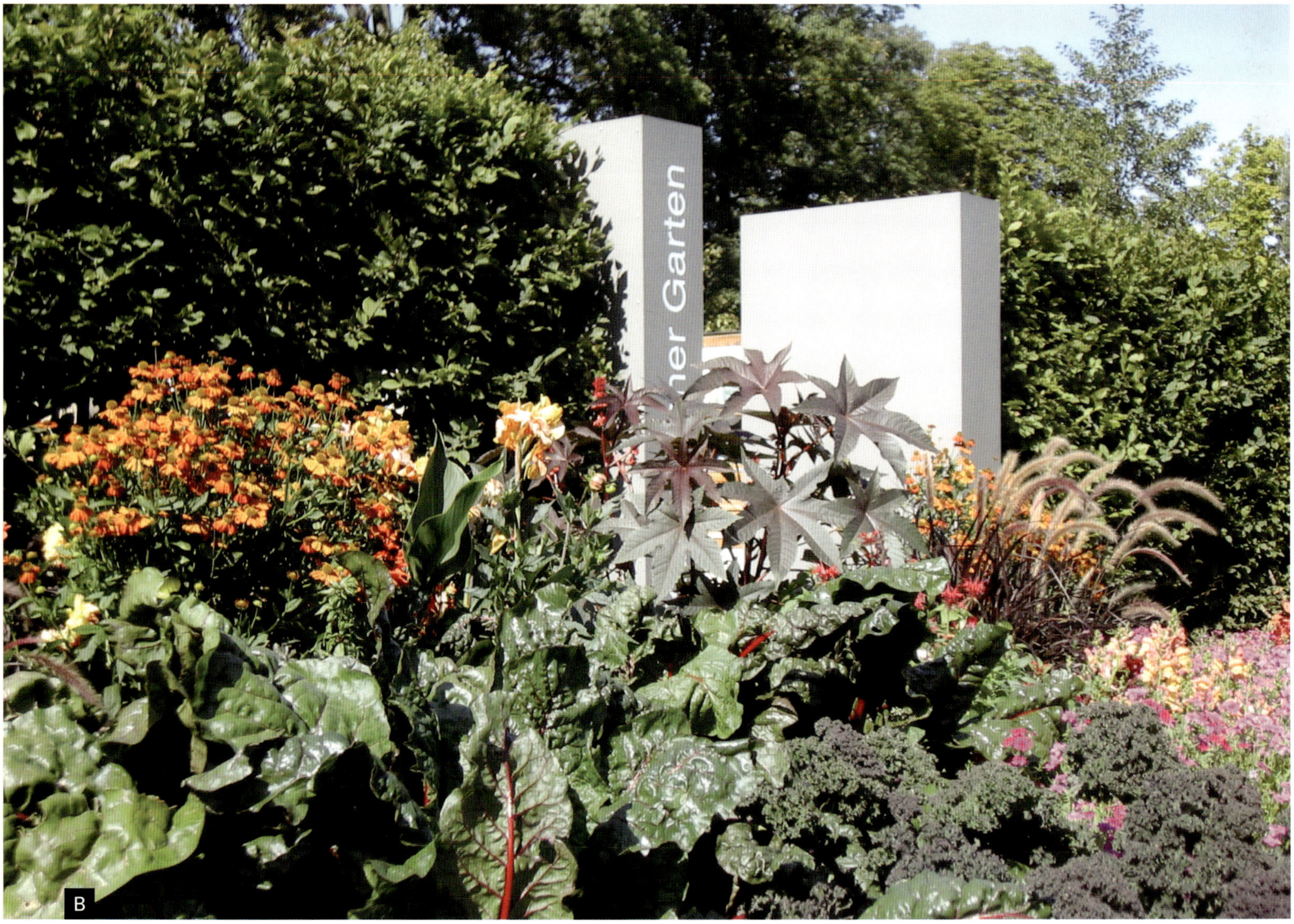

B

C

A between hedge gardens

B gate of hedge gardens

C hegde garden of succulents

A the park as important basis of the new quarter
B a thematic designed playground

Carlebach Park

Landcape:	Levin Monsigny Landschaftsarchitekten
Location:	Lübeck, Germany
Client:	HEG Hochschulstadtteil-Entwicklungsgesellschaft mbH
Completion:	2005
Size:	57.000 m²
Costs:	3.300.000 €
Photographs:	Claas Dreppenstedt

A

The starting point for the design of University Quarter in Lübeck is the symmetrical layout of the historical hospital complex. The hospital's central axis acts as a reference, giving form to the central open space: the new District Park. This park connects the treatment wards of the hospital, the campus and the adjacent neighbourhood, and as such becomes the hub and busy interface for people in the area. This combination and multi-functionality are the best prerequisites for a thriving open space.

An essential characteristic of the design for the new park is the way in which the trees are used to produce a number of different effects. The trees help to define the central space, drawing attention to the central axis and its role within the context of the wider city fabric. Their planning is shaped by the influences at work within the immediate surroundings: a "splintering" of the adjoining areas, asymmetrical edges and differing intensities of development. By their particular arrangement they organize the large overall area of the park into comprehensible units, emphasising and defining differing states of density and emptiness, which in turn suggest how these individual spaces may be used.

The resultant area includes elements characteristic of a classical open space: the expansive esplanade on the north side of the park faces a promenade on the southern edge; in between a bowling green with generous lawns set aside for a variety of different uses; a lively tree-covered university campus and the reflective calm of the hospital park at the eastern end.

Ultimately, it is the use of trees which unites the park structure over its entire length into a spatial continuum: the various spatial and functional relationships between the areas shape the identity of the new district park. The arrangement and composition of the open spaces, despite the use of traditional elements, result in an unmistakably contemporary park which nonetheless meets the demands put upon it.

A master plan, location in the urban space

B bright concrete block stairs terrace the lawn up
   to the Esplanade

A

B

C

A the gardens of power: kingcup garden
B the gardens of power: kingkup garden
and lindenwood garden

BUGA Munich 2005

Landscape:	Rainer Schmidt Landschaftsarchitekten
Architect:	Reinhard Bauer, Munich
Location:	Munich Riem, Germany
Client:	Bundesgartenschau München 2005 GmbH
Completion:	2005
Size:	130 ha
Costs:	13.000.000 €
Photographs:	Stefan Mueller Naumann

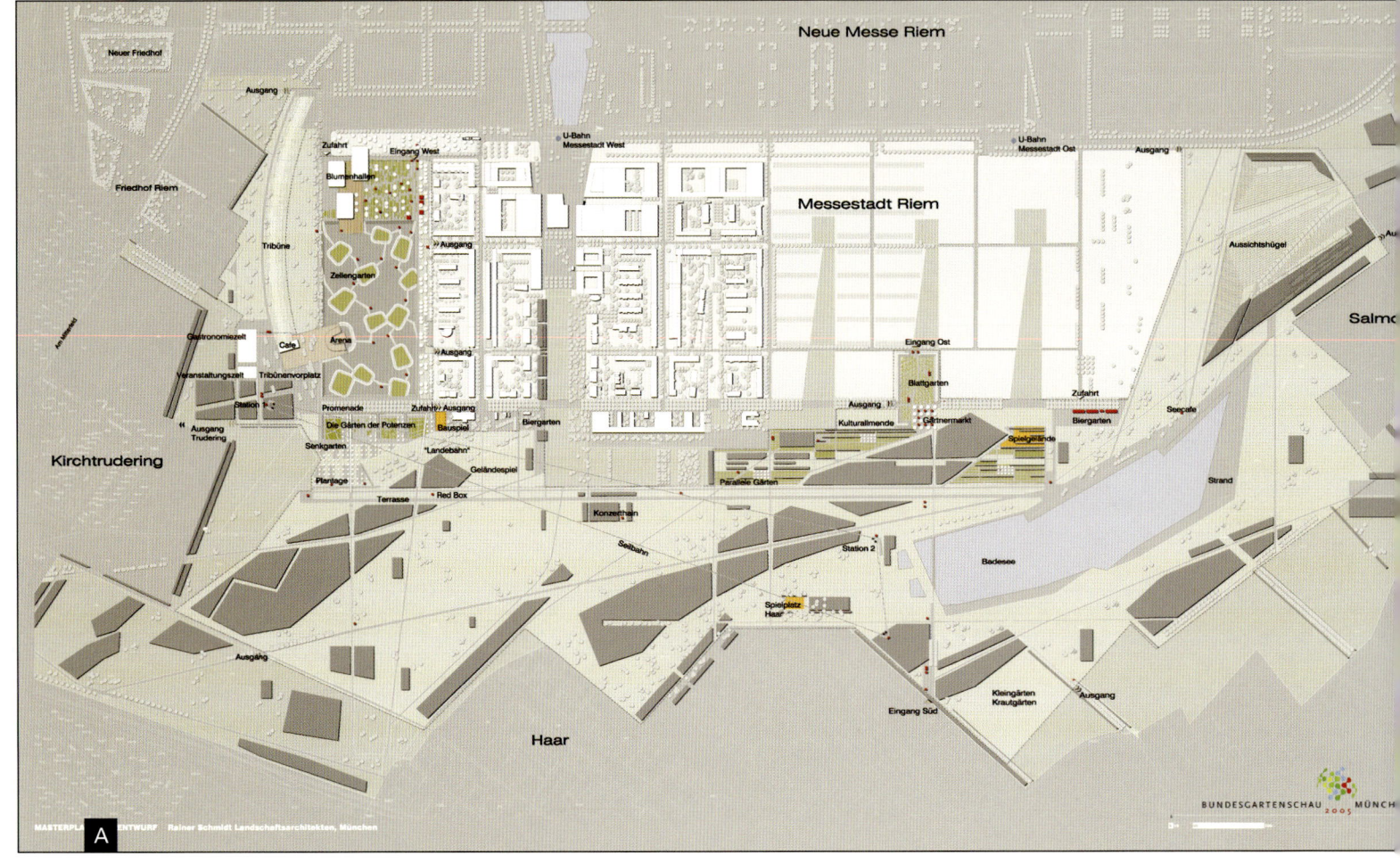

The existing park with its generous way connections, meadows areas and thickets represents an essential attraction point. Therefore the Buga (Federal Garden Exhibition) planning fewer changes for the south part of the landscape park. The live in the park with a various of micro structure will be comes more a central part of this exhibition. Mobile cams send pictures out of the park live to a kind of Red-Boxes which can find along the exhibition area and open visitors a new perspective views. These micro and macro views of the park live are based in the Buga concept as inspiration. The organic forms – as structural basic pattern of all vegetables life – became to the basic form topic of the central exhibition terrain. The exhibit flowers and plants will present in original form.

The production of change of the perspective, the micro and macro, stretches along as a red thread of different articulation through the total BUGA-terrain. The garden show becomes the bridge for further unaccustomed perception of landscape architecture, nature and plant.

The typical materiality of the existing interim areas in Riem becomes to the design basic: gravel heap form the cell garden and frame the leaf garden. That temporarily character of the garden show no contradiction to the sustainability, but rather it is as an incentive to understand for an unorthodox solution.

| A master plan BUGA |
| B cell gardens - overview |
| C master plan the gardens of power |

A

B

A the gardens of power: alga garden

B sunkengarden - garden of tiliatree

C the cell gardens - animal track garden

A view of Chadar Cascade
B aerial of the Diana, Princess of Wales Memorial Fountain

Diana Princess of Wales Memorial

Landscape: Gustafson Porter Ltd.
Location: Hyde Park, London
Client: Department of Culture, Media and Sport
Completion: 2004
Photographs: Helene Binet, Texxus, Gustafson Porter

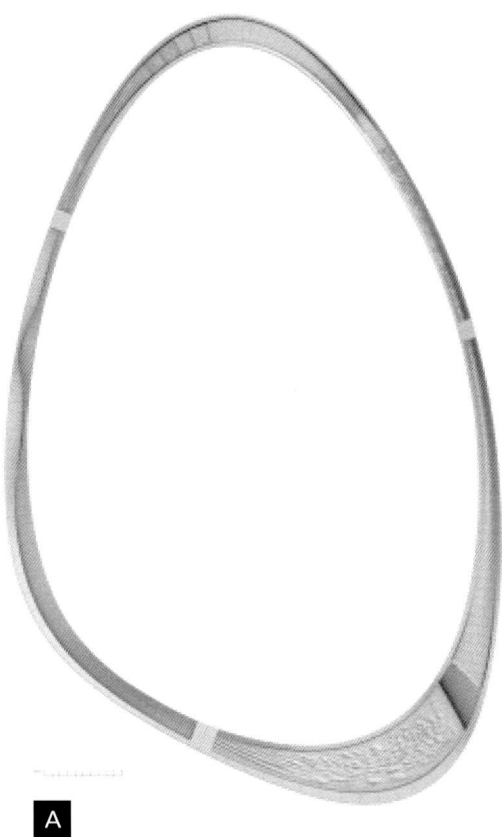

A

The design for the Diana, Princess of Wales Memorial Fountain by Gustafson Porter went through a number of key stages. It began with the designers' first model of the Memorial and their description of the complex textures, patterns and water features on its surface that would make the water tumble, cascade, curl and bubble as it ran its course. It also involved the development of the hydraulic design of the various water jets in collaboration with Arup engineers. The challenge was to make this vision into a technically deliverable program of work.

Initially, a clay model was created by designers Kathryn Gustafson and Neil Porter. As well as modeling the fountain, it also incorporated the reworking of the land around the fountain in Hyde Park. Once completed, a rubber mould of the clay model was created and a cast from the mould was digitally scanned by the Ford Motor Company to create a 'three-dimensional scan file'. The Ford 'scan file' allowed the design team to create sections through the Memorial's granite ring and surrounding landform to develop the design of the features in more detail. This was the first time that this software had been used for architectural purposes - it had to be adapted from its usual automotive industry applications.

Surface Development & Engineering (SDE), a British firm specializing in high quality computer generated surface models were able to develop the design from Gustafson Porter into the final smooth 3D model. They used their computers to model the full shape of the Memorial, creating a seamless electronic file detailing the exact shape and location of each of the 545 stones in the Memorial. This file, referred to as a 'jelly mould', could then be divided into individual 'virtual' blocks for the stonecutters.

The outcome of this groundbreaking technical effort was a set of complex computer files that described, with engineering accuracy, the precise shape and surface texture of each piece of stone in the Memorial. At the same time one key area of the Memorial, known as the 'swoosh', was built in mock up by Imperial College, London. This was used in trials to fine tune the spectacular water effects at this key section. Another mock-up was produced, by water feature specialists Ocmis, of the 'bubbles' introduced into the western side of the fountain.

B view of Diana, Princess of Wales Memorial Fountain looking South

C view of Diana, Princess of Wales Memorial Fountain looking North

A Diana Memorial Fountain Layout Master

B view of Diana, Princess of Wales Memorial Fountain looking South

C view of Diana, Princess of Wales Memorial Fountain looking North

A

C

A stepped Cascade Section

B detail of Chadar Cascade

C stepped Cascade Section with running water

A

B

A steel meridian crossing
B bench at Finow Canal

State Horticultural Garden Show Eberswalde

Landscape:	TOPOTEK 1
Location:	Eberswalde, Germany
Client:	City of Eberswalde
Completion:	2002
Size:	17 ha
Costs:	5.000.000 €
Photographs:	Hanns Joosten

Adjacent to the Finow Canal a former industrial site dating from the early nineteenth century was cleared and converted into a new type of park. The concept for the transformation of this early industrial area focuses less on heightening the experience of industrial romanticism and more on offering orientation, mapping the site as a post-industrial landscape park. The park contrasts intensive areas of experience with the vastness of space. The uniquely-designed park lavishes details ranging from picturesque situations to urban graphics on a tarmac. The existing elements of the site were not connected in terms of hierarchy or location but rather through a dynamic grid. The vast, former industrial site is mapped as a post-industrial park by a system of paths; forty-centimetre-wide steel tapes run through the terrain describing wide radii, most of them accompanied by paths. The steel tapes span the whole of the new park like a geographical map grid of meridians and parallels. They define—and make visible—the expanse of the terrain shaped and re-shaped by the old industrial works over the course of its history.

The elaboration of the spatial potential includes both the accentuation of topographical situations and the interpretive conceptual development of extant elements. For example, the subterranean canals formerly used to cool the rolling mills were opened for pedal boats. This spatial archaeology forms the third component in the multi-faceted cultural landscape of the new park.

Showcase
A chain of highly-detailed exhibition gardens at the entrance area of the park forms a design-image intended to provide a spatial and thematic contrast to the expanse of the landscape park in the Finow Valley. These densely-concentrated gardens form a conceptual sequel to the nineteenth-century museum cabinets in which curios were collected for the visitors' amusement. This string of plots is a central element of the garden exhibition and consists of rectangular thematic gardens of approximately 150 square meters. They form showcases for their discrete little worlds with different staging a blossoming, odorous, ever-changing collection of garden objects placed in a consciously artificial manner in the park. For example, the "garden of the senses" displays the effect which scented plants have on the physical and spiritual well-being of mankind; the medical garden, in which the appropriate healing plants are located at the relevant part of a body represented in silhouette on the ground, conveys physical knowledge. The vital sequence of spaces between the showcases reveal the constantly changing correlation between the gardens during the waxing and waning of the growing season.

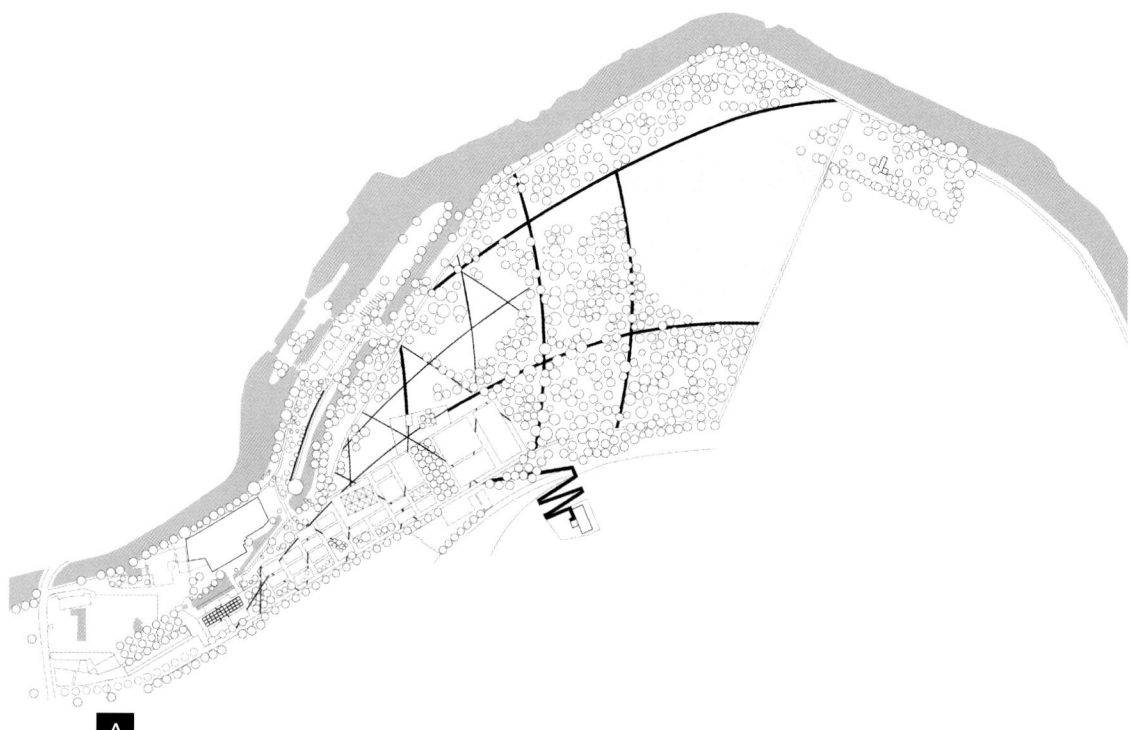

A

B

C

A master plan

B Jesus Walk On Water - Watergarden

C Chill Out Garden

A

B

A path in the postindustrial park

B band of Show Gardens

C postindustrial park

B

A wooden footbridge through the unspoilt natural environment
B footbridge through field of reeds

IGA - International Garden Exhibition Rostock

Landscape:	**WES & Partner** Wehberg Schatz Betz Kaschke Landscape architects
Location:	Rostock, Germany
Client:	IGA Rostock 2003 GmbH and City of Rostock
Completion:	2003
Size:	900.000 m²
Costs:	35.790.400 €
Photographs:	WES & Partner

The International Landscaping and Gardening Exhibition held in Rostock, Germany is a horticultural show, and fair but also a park for the general public. It will be evolve in the riverbed on the banks of the Warnow, between the Rostock neighbourhoods of Groß-Klein and Schmarl. This marshland region is still impressive even though feeder streams have now deteriorated into gullies and the winding bends of the streams have disappeared. That is why we want to revisit the landscape as it once was in the parts of the new park. A rural landscape that is suggestive of Arcadia while exuding peace and sparseness in its monochromatic expanse of reeds and wide expanse of meadows. The existing and rediscovered landscape is the agenda – it forms the underlying framework for the world we will create. The blend of these two characters makes us aware of the aesthetic value of both.

A overview of urban planning for international horticultural exhibition

B concept for undulating bridge through meadows

C cable car above the Klostergraben

D meadow with Allium bulb flowers

C

D

A

B

C

A slope with roses

B Klostergraben bridge in natural meadow area

C Warnow riverbank with cable car

A

B

A pioneer vegetation on a sun-exposed slope
B arial view of the spoil heap under construction

Grosses Holz Spoil Heap

Landscape:	Planungsbüro Drecker
Location:	Germany
Client:	Deutsche Steinkohle AG
Completion:	1st phase of construction 2004/2005
Size:	1.200.000 m²
Costs:	2.700.000 €
Photographs:	Peter Drecker, Katrin Zimmermann

The planning area lies in a mining district, in which wide swathes of countryside have been altered by coal mining. The Grosses Holz Spoil Heap, too, is a "landscape construction" - built by accumulation of material displaced by mining. The heap forms the highest point in the countryside surrounding the two cities of Unna and Bergkamen, and it has developed into a much-visited location. But this landmark serves not only as a local recreational facility; it also creates new habitats for animals and plants.

The tree plateau incorporates the principle of the heap in a flat countryside. Deep-set groves of trees are incised into the body of the heap. Raised groves extend out of the plateau. They mark polygonal bases which, following the form of dried, torn open earth extending across the plain. The interplay of positive and negative volumes en-hances the unnatural effect of the topography, making it comprehensible at the same time. The choice of plants reflects the adjacent vegetation of extreme habitats. They are grouped by their features such as grey leaves, autumn colours or white spring blossoms.

A ramp connects the tree plateau with further design elements: the natural arena and the grass plateau, enclosed by grass banks. The grass plateau is characterised by a grid of differently coloured grasses. The peculiar shapes emphasise the unnatural character of the heap landscape.

Grosses Holz is an example of how an everyday landscape can be developed - the results of regular mining have become a starting point for a cultural landscape of the post-industrial era.

A illustrative site plan

B retention of surface water and development of wetland habitats on the Tree Plateau

C view of the Natural Arena (amphitheatre) under construction

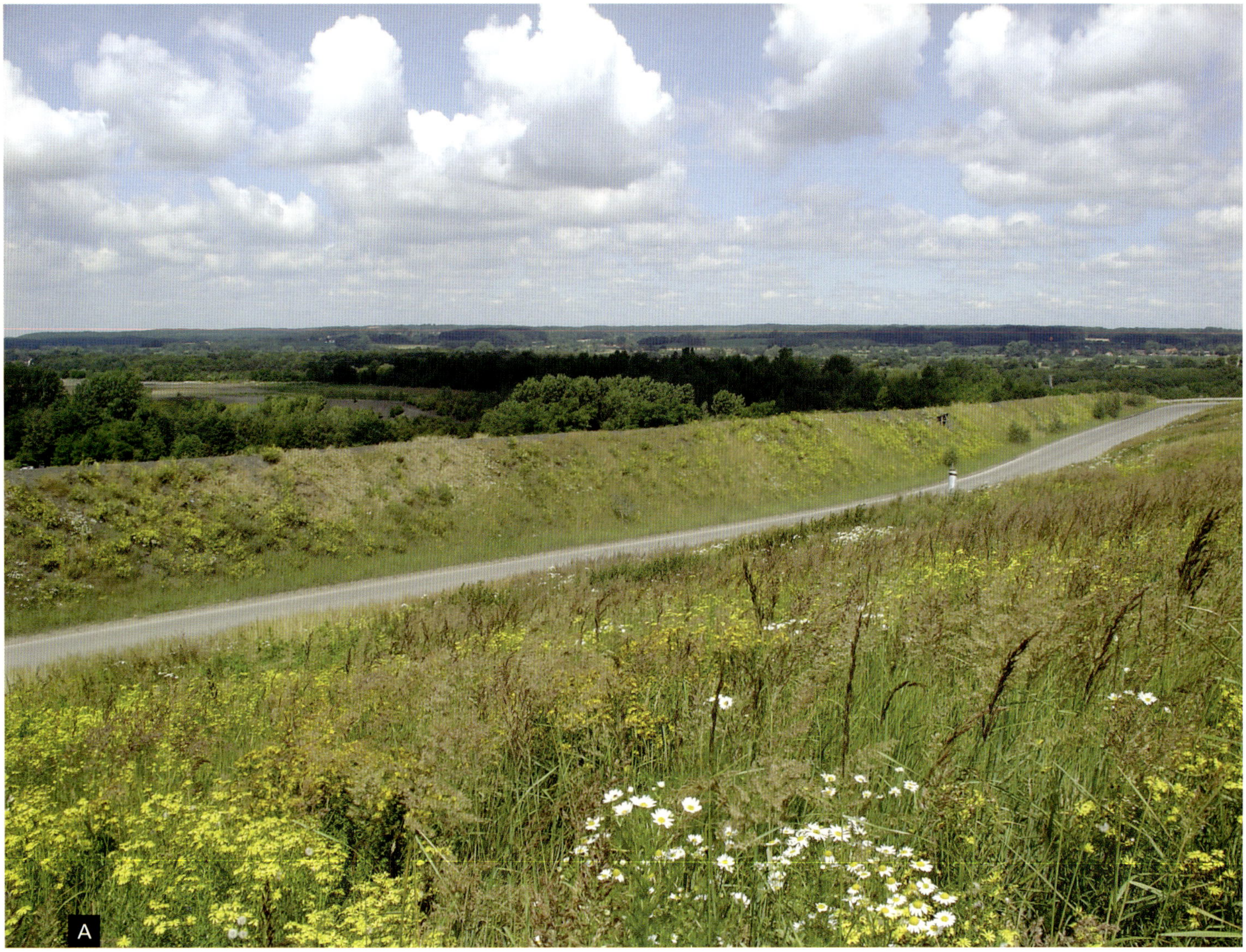
A

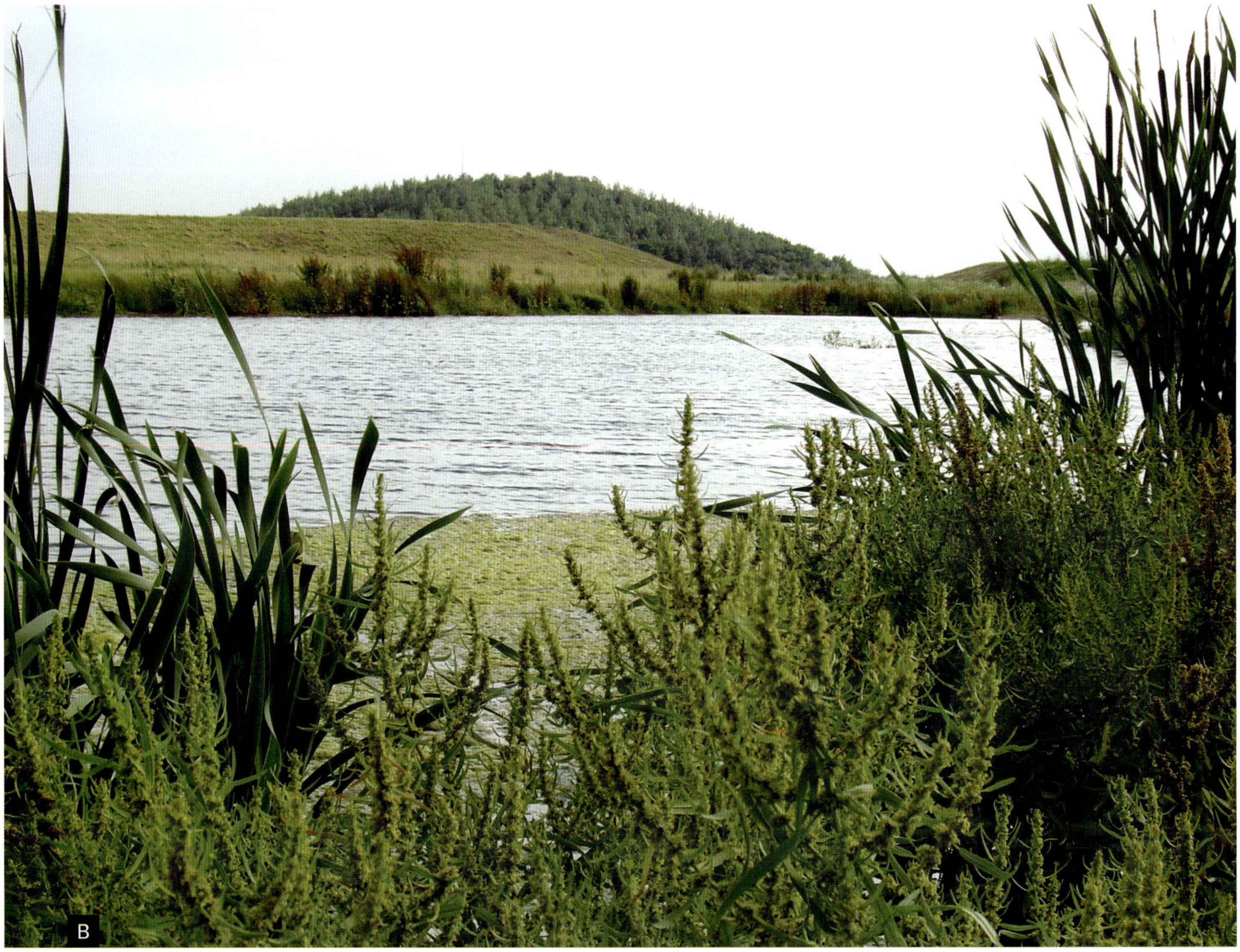
B

C

A view from top of the spoil heap into the
surrounding cultural landscape with its typical
mosaic of woods and farmland ("Münsterland")

B artificial topography on the heap

C contrast between cultivated nature and
industrial landscape

B

A room of echo with a well containing a sound by speaking
B stone room with sand and different stones

Garden of Knowledge

Landscape:	Monika Gora
Co-worker:	Caroline Kindstrand
Location:	Västra Hamnen, Malmö, Sweden
Client:	Municipality of Malmö
Completion:	2001
Size:	2000 m^2
Costs:	150 000 €
Photographs:	Urszula Striner, Monika Gora

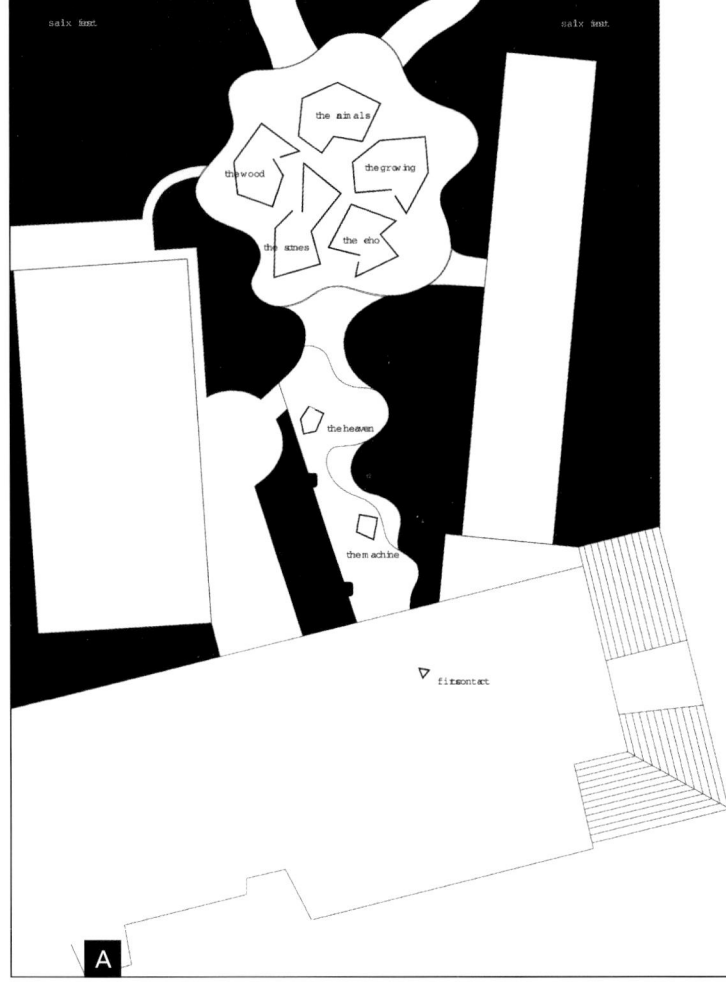

Once I heard a lecture about an Indian people who used the word " maize" not only as a name of their basic food but also as an over all concept for everything here in the world. Everything. Everything that exists and everything they experienced.

If you imagine that everything can be called"maize" the whole universe becomes potential food. We convert the world through our bodies – whether through the digestion system or through the digestion system or through feelings, attitudes, experiences. At the same time we are someone else's"maize". Our surroundings leave their marks on us and we on them. Seeing the whole world as food is an approach without fear. Everything can be converted and used, broken down into some kind of sustenance.

I see this elementary interpretation of the world order as a flow of sustenance as a very apt description of the world order as a flow of sustenance as a very apt description of the nature of knowledge when they literally swallow everything in their knowledge; children's enduring, unendurable way of conquering their knowledge when they literally swallow everything in their zeal to explore the world. No element of the work is left to anyone else. Can by myself, must by myself. Taste everything at all costs.

No matter how many times I hurt myself. Taste and accept or reject. All this becomes blunted, as we know , when the experience bank of adulthood grows and sink in. Fearful of consuming incorrectly or to much, we become selective and inclined to limit our intake of experience.

In the Garden of Knowledge there is plenty of "maize" for everyone. Here it is isn't about what's correct but about daring to accept and convert what flows towards you. Testing, feeling, tasting, trying, seeing, hearing. In other worlds taking it all in with all your senses, with your whole body, assimilating the flow, digesting, ejecting the surplus.

A site plan

B Garden of Knowledge is surrounded by a forest of willow

C entering the area. View towards the labyrinth of the five main rooms

B

C

A room with a pine tree and different woods

B view from one of the "castles in the air",
   all the walls are timbered

C third small room with a water tap, water closet
   and the sky above to watch

D room of growth – with fast growing plants

E "Castles in the air" – towers in different heights
   made of steel, wood and hay

A

A folly "Water-island" with perspective along the fish-pond to the castle and the heights of Harz-mountains

B theme garden: "Parterre" with a view to the "Magical-wood"

Wernigerode State Horticultural Show 2006

Landscape:	hutterreimann + cejka Landschaftsarchitektur
Architect:	A_lab architektur, Jens Schmahl
Location:	Wernigerode, Germany
Client:	City of Wernigerode
Completion:	2006
Size:	35 ha
Costs:	8,700.000 €
Photographs:	Franziska Poreski, Christo Libuda

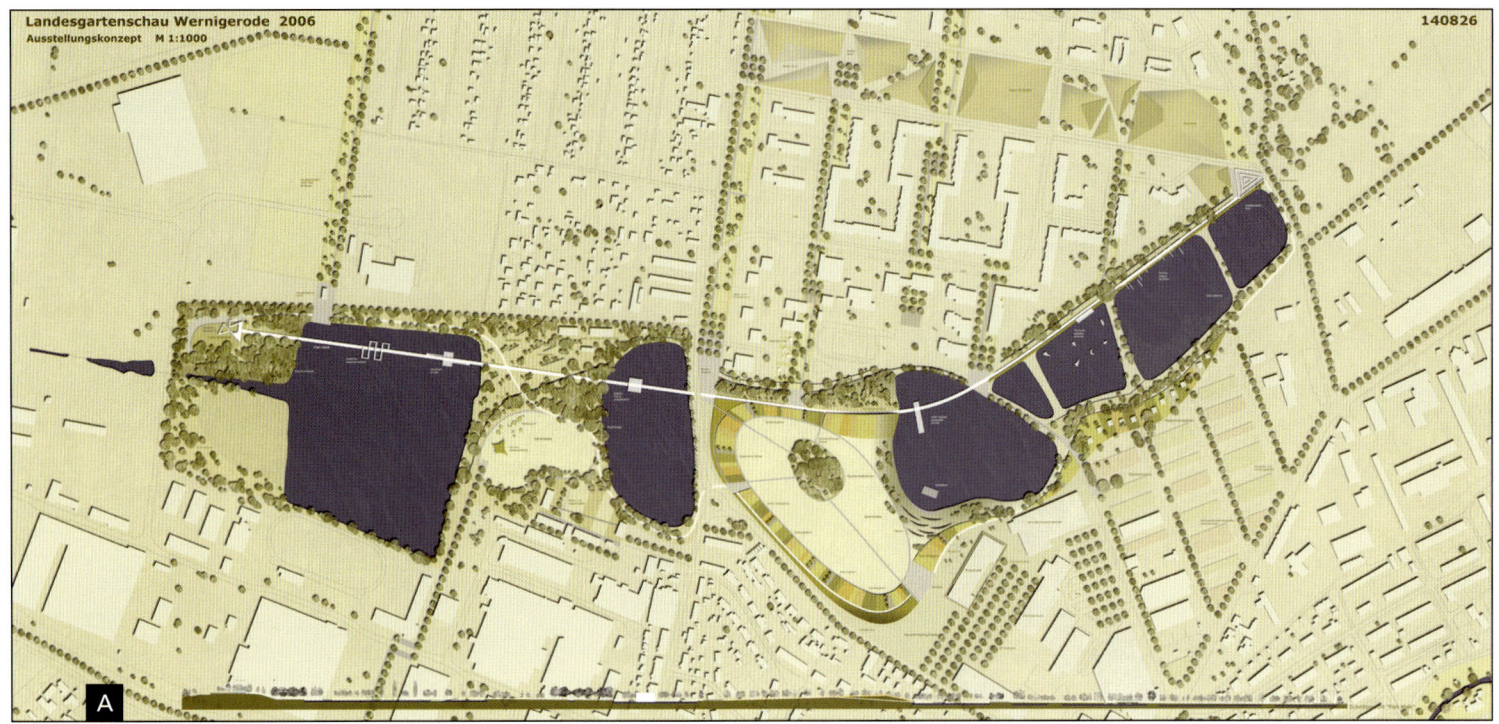

A

The seven historical fishponds on the edge of the town of Wernigerode near the northern Harz Mountain provide the setting of the garden festival 2006.

Enclosed by industrial- and farm land, blocks of prefabricated flats and allotments the existing landscape has a disjointed quality, the ponds being spatially separated from each other.

The project makes visible the locations hidden qualities without erasing the vestiges of history.

A walkway running 1.000m from east to west - the "Fish Walk" - links the ponds. Along the walkway come the so-called "Follies", designed as architectural features for walking along, planned by the office of A-lab architektur, and providing a stage for water as an element. They serve to create a mood, to provide points of pleasure, drawing attention to themselves, attractions both during and after the horticultural show. The "Follies" are various things - a waterfall for walking through, a translucent aquarium, showing the various stages of fish breeding, a media-art event showroom for virtual underwater life, or just large seats in the water. More than this the "Fish Walk" is a "Mineral Gorge", cutting deeply into the landfill, making it a geological nature trail, from the foothill of the Harz to its mountainous heights. Along the ponds, where there was once a dump for waste building materials, winds the "Garden Strip", a series of 40 theme gardens. Look out for the "Recycling Gardens", in which building materials and demolition waste in combination with plants are turned into design elements. The gardens are bordering a wide meadow, taking the "Magic wood" in its center. This is framed by a shining ribbon of perforated metal; sparkling treasures evoke the legend of the Wernigerode dwarfs. The gently curving "Landscape Promenade" provides a subtle counterpart to the brash linearity of the "Fish Walk". Thus a modern park has been created, displaying its own special regional features in the balancing act between show and sustainable use.

A master plan

B the "Mineral Gorge"

A folly "Water-island"

B the "Scout" offers Natural Views

C a place to be at the Folly: "Landing stage"

D the "Mineral-gorge" cutts through the landfill
of the former waste dump

A

B

A steel plant containers and cafe in the courtyard
B dark bands of natural stone through the lane

Marstall Square Munich – Stage for Urban Life

Landscape:	ST raum a. landscape architecture
Architect	Gewers Kühn & Kühn Architekten
Location:	Munich, Germany
Client:	Dreyer Brettel & Kollegen Management GmbH
Completion:	2004
Size:	2,2 ha
Costs:	1,800.000 €
Photographs:	Marcus Bredt

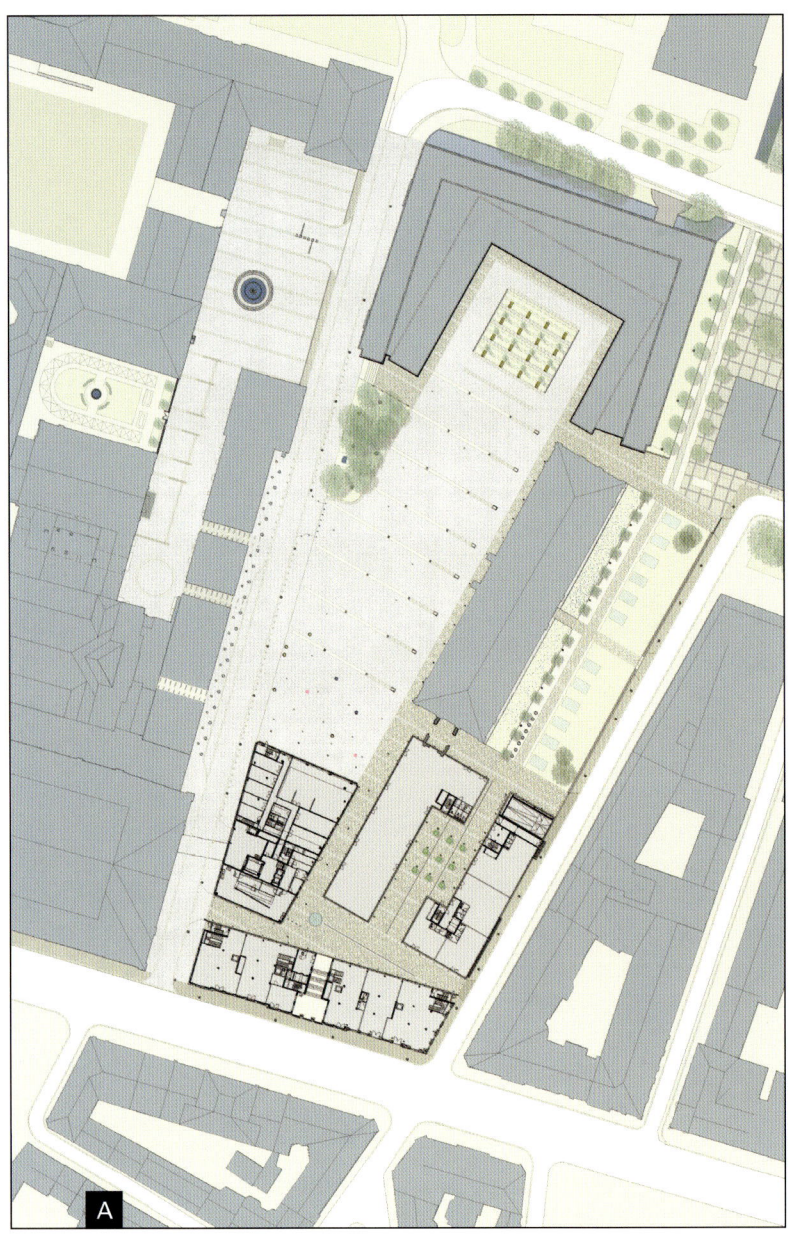

An urban space with expressive clarity was created to meet the demands of a historic major city. The whole complex of the Marstallplatz including Salpeterhof [Salpeter courtyard], Maximilianhof [Maximilian courtyard] and the eastern part of the front court of the residency were paved with granite in alternating formats. Dark bands of natural stone cover the squares and courtyards. Three fountains enliven the ensemble, in particular the plain dark granite fountain basin where water bubbles invitingly in the Salpeterhof. The unique in-laid lights bring the Marstallplatz to life at night while, the ground-level spotlights near the building emphasize the architecture. The various open space elements are connected through narrow lanes and passages and are thus integrated into the existing urban structure. The "stone-covered" Marstallplatz is the stage for urban life, festivities and concerts in Munich.

A master plan

B stone water fountian in the Salpeterhof

C illuminated steps at the church courtyard

B

C

A illuminated Marstall Square

B restored Kronprinz-Rupprecht fountain

C a stone surface covers the Marstall Square

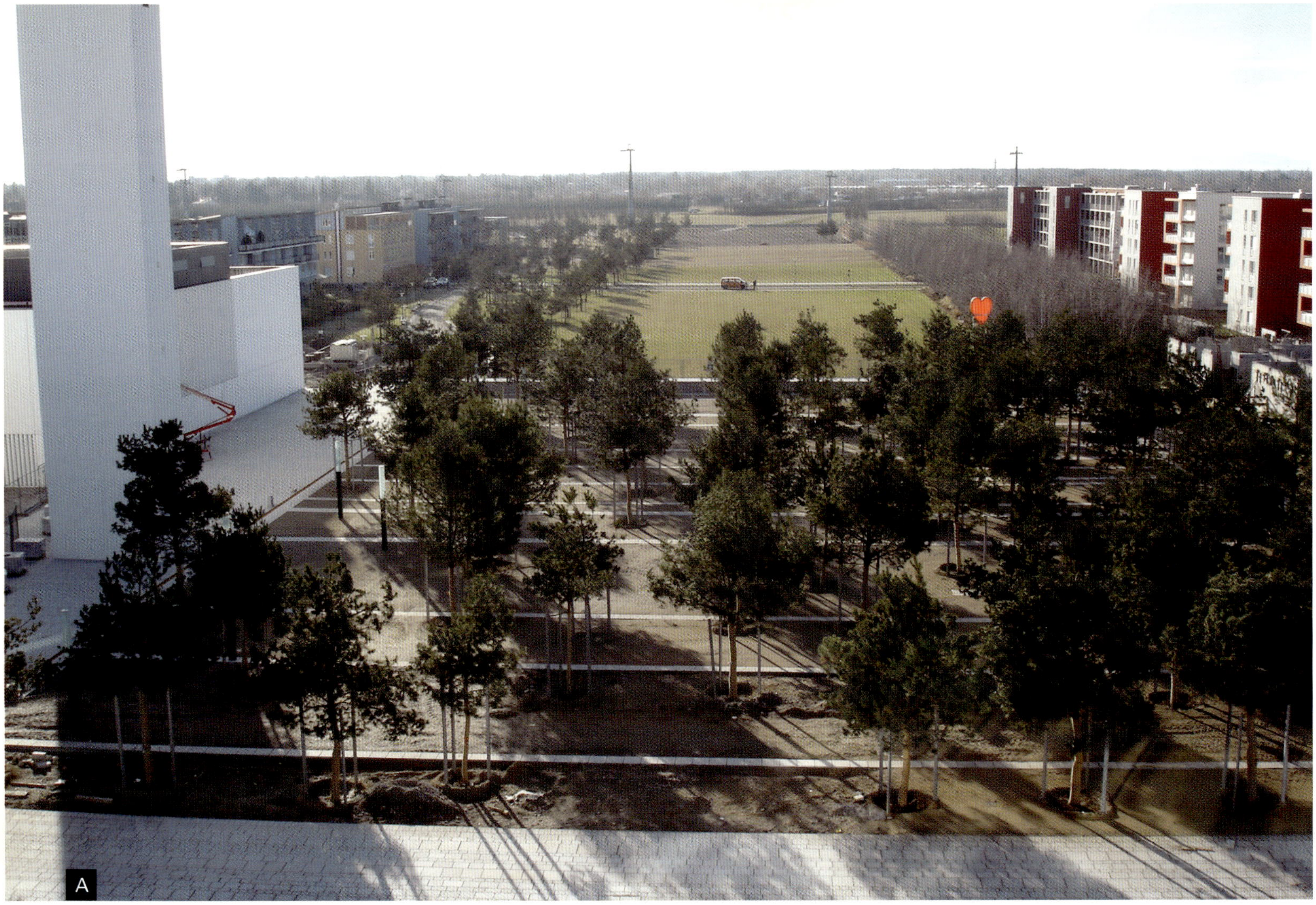

A

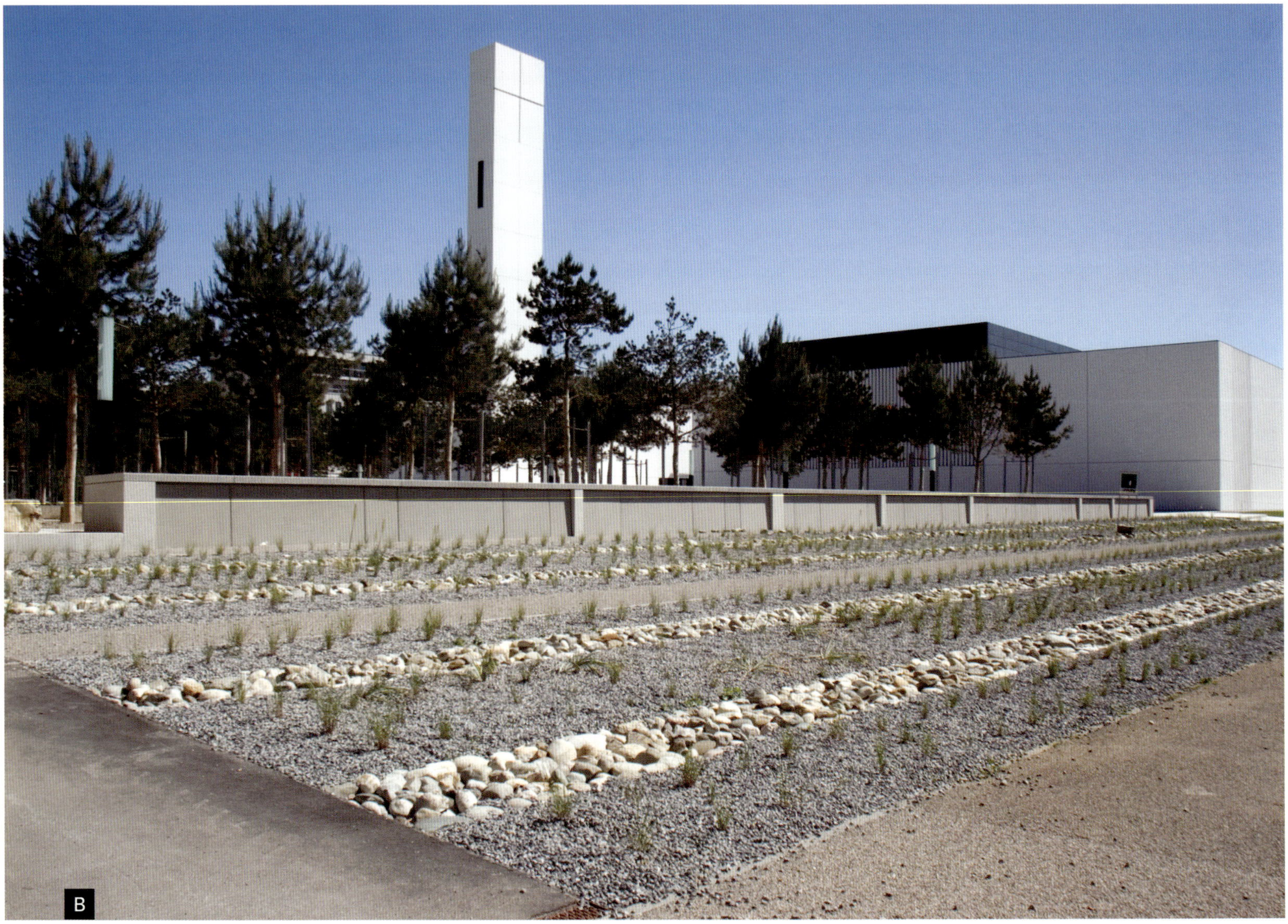

B

C

A overview from the surrounding buildings
B view of the 'city balcony' from the central green corridor
C view from the coffee bar terrace to the plaza

Plaza of the Human Rights

Architect:	Valentien + Valentien
Location:	Munich Riem, Germany
Client:	City of Munich
Completion:	2005
Size:	13000 m^2
Cost:	3.500.000 €
Photographs:	Horst Burger, Michael Latz,
	Valentien + Valentien

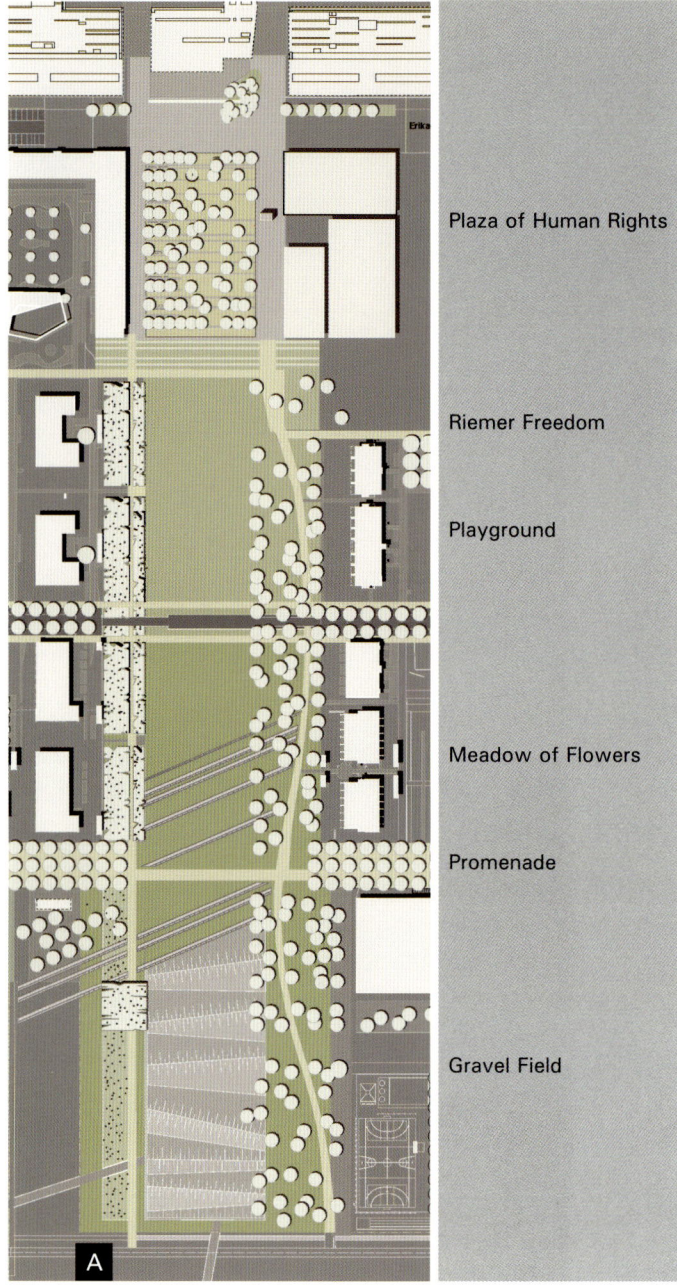

Plaza of Human Rights

Riemer Freedom

Playground

Meadow of Flowers

Promenade

Gravel Field

A

The urban design concept for the Trade Fair City of Riem organizes the quarter through a hierarchical system of public places and green areas. The north-south directional green corridor provides attractive and traffic-free pathways that connect almost all residential structures with the new landscape park. The broader central green corridor is part of a network of public areas and provides a visual and structural connection from Trade Fair Plaza to the Plaza of the Human Rights and on to the landscape park, thus functioning as an important orientation and axle for the entire quarter. The surrounding narrow green corridors serve as recreational areas for the adjacent residential neighbourhoods. The broad, tree-covered promenade forms the southern delineation of the Trade Fair City. Here, important infrastructure facilities such as schools and kindergartens form the prelude to the landscape park.

A	master plan
B	oak logs in the shade of pine trees
C	long bench within a group of birches

B

C

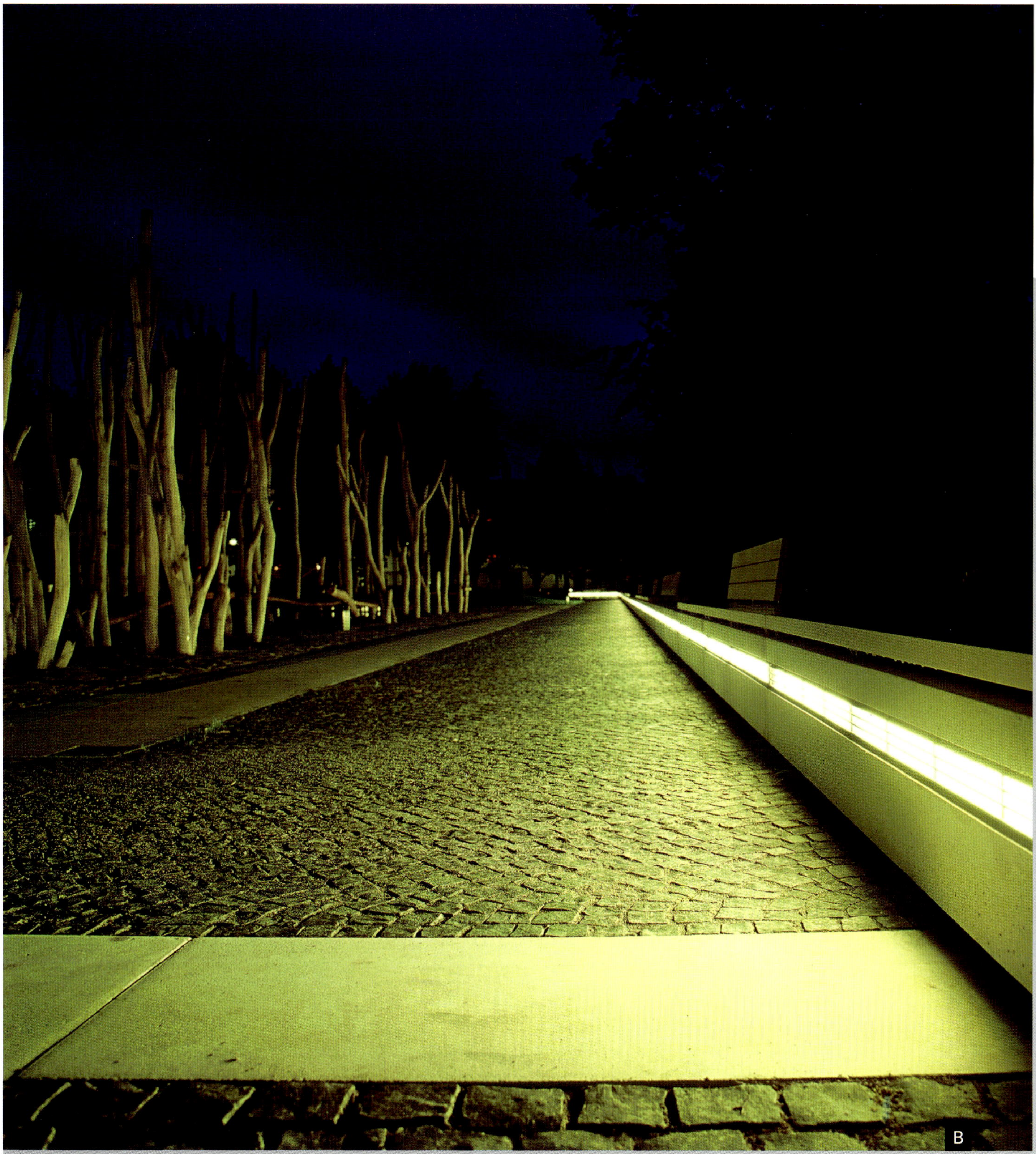

B

Georg-Freundorfer Plaza

Landscape:	Levin Monsigny Landschaftsarchitekten
Location:	Munich, Germany
Client:	City of Munich, Public Construction Authority
Completion:	2002
Size:	18.000 m^2
Costs:	1.600.000 €
Photographs:	Claas Dreppenstedt

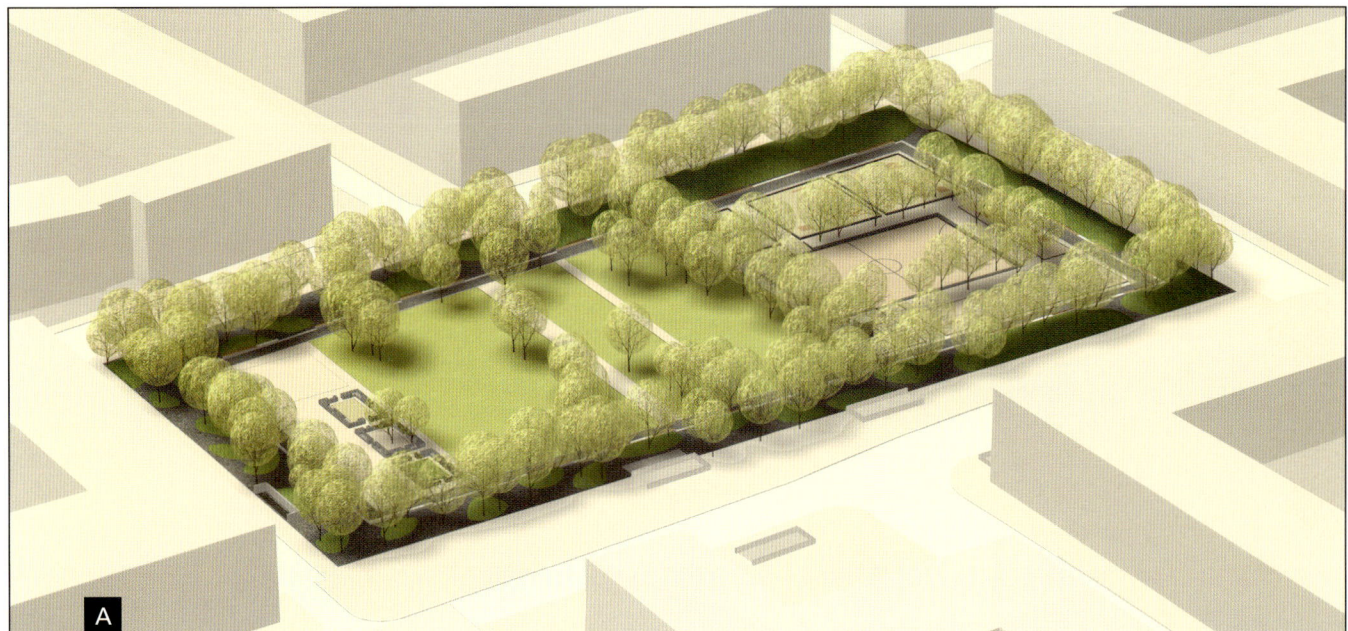

A

The Georg Freundorfer Plaza is located in the Westend District of Munich, a traditional working class area. Its perimeter development structure, built in the late 19th century, made it the highest density residential area in the city. New housing projects are now being built on the neighboring Theresienhöhe, the former exhibition grounds. The Georg Freundorfer Plaza thus plays an important role as a meeting place for local residents, as a space for public events and as a multi-functional area for rest and recreation. Created in the 1960's as a playground, its high earthen banks overgrown with big trees form a barrier between the plaza and the residential area. The new design for the plaza had to integrate the existing trees, and therefore the existing topography, and at the same time re-establish the lost connection to the surrounding urban area.

The Georg Freundorfer Plaza was given a functional and visual frame, uniting a plaza dissected by various functions and design elements. This frame furthermore helps to define the accessibility of the plaza both internally and with the city. It is a permeable membrane.
A fine, light band accentuates the frame and divides the basalt pavement into a narrow strip of small pavers and a wide strip of medium-sized pavers. The band occasionally rises and serves as seating from which one can observe the plaza's lively activities. Integrated lighting follows the rhythm of the band and makes the plaza's newly regained dimensions visible even at night. Earthen mounds rise up over the frame, dominating the northern part of the plaza and yet allowing for several points of access. Towards the Theresienwiese to the south the mounds taper down, diminishing in size until they are mere green spots on the dark basalt paving material of the frame. Underneath the protective canopy of the trees and amidst abundant plantings of shade-loving ground covers, ferns and ornamental grasses, they welcome local residents and passers-by to the plaza.

B

C

A site plan, location in the urban space

B the framing path

C paved area as residential meeting place

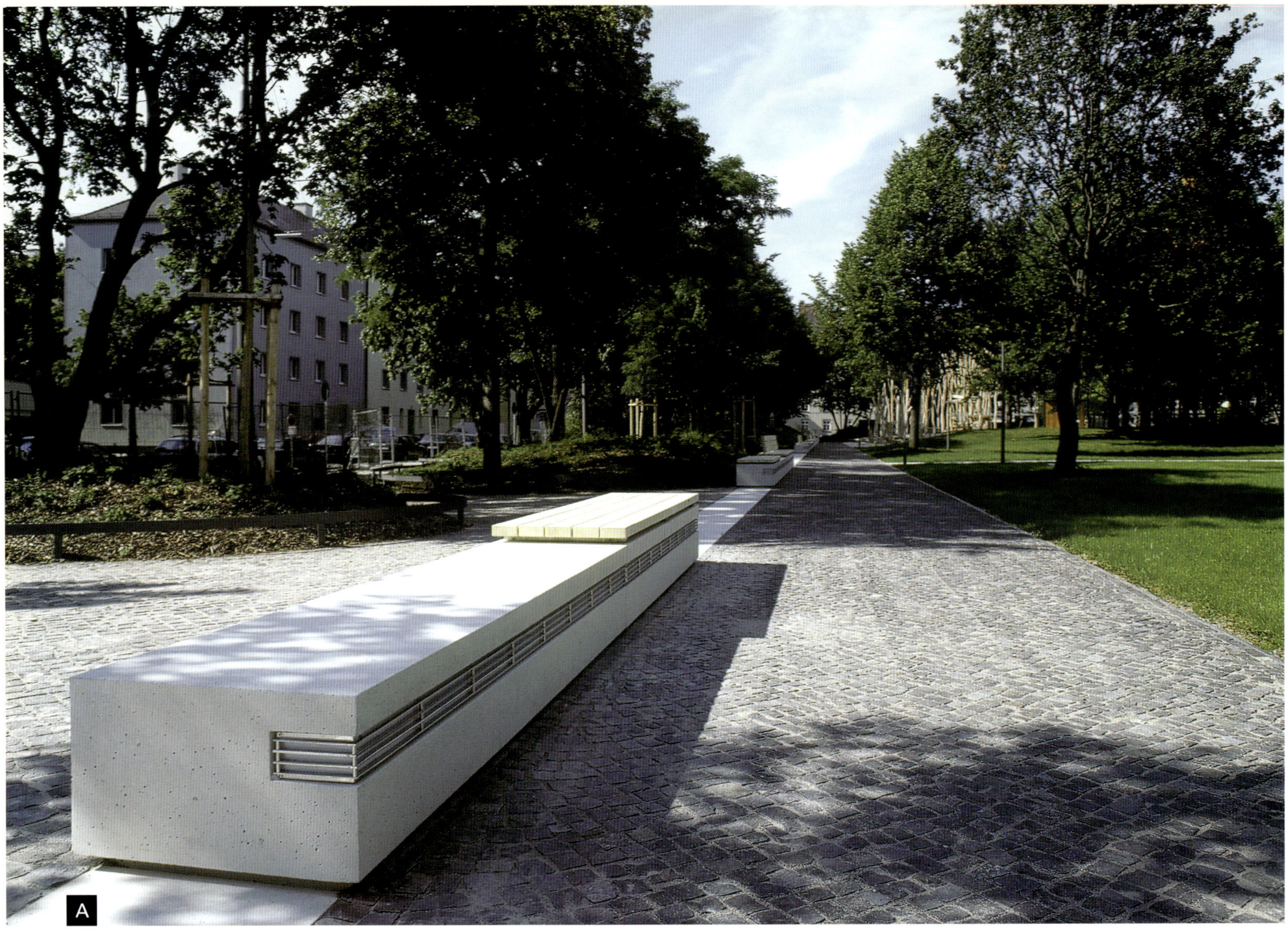

A

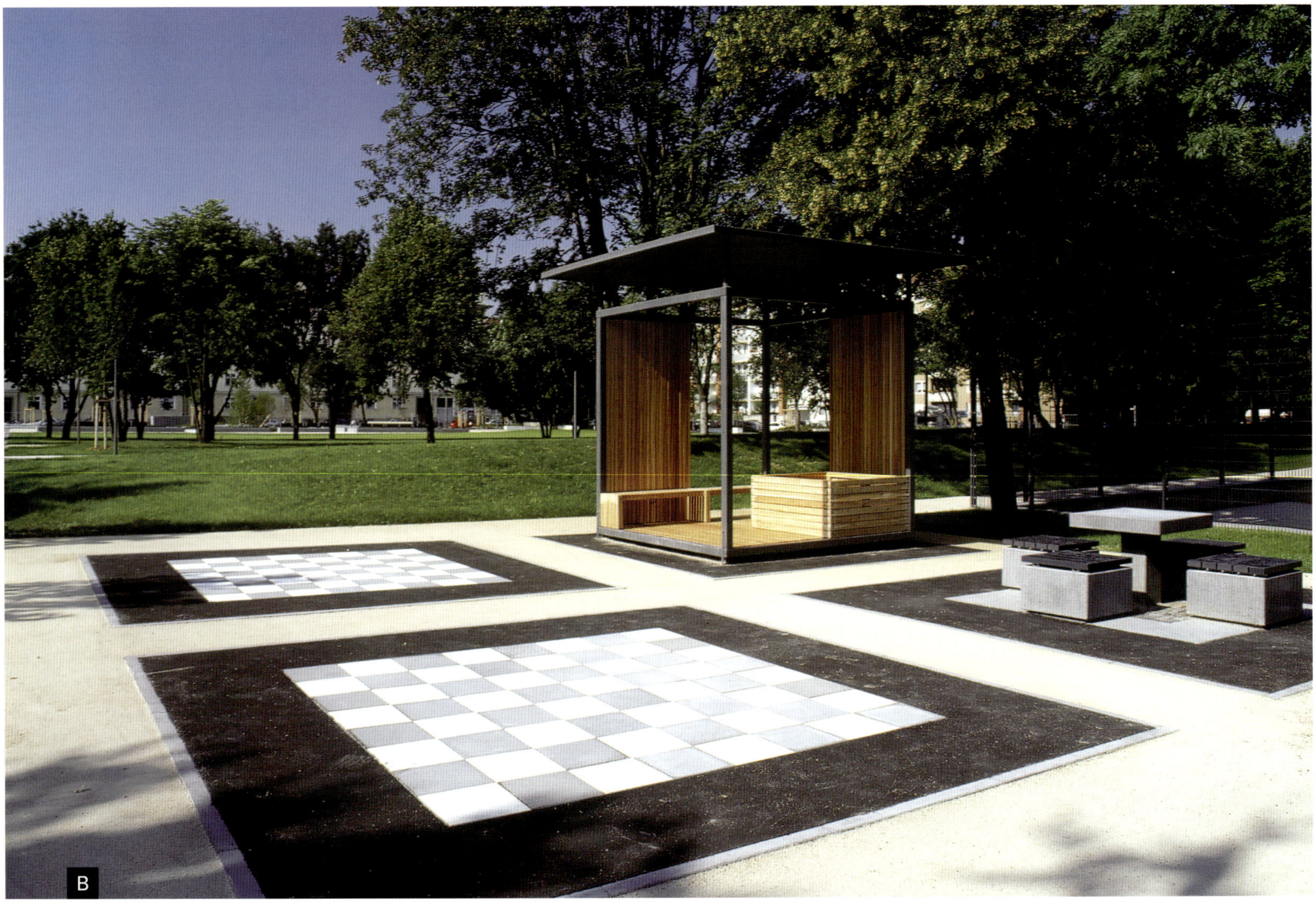

B

A-B	the alternation of light and dark is visible in all details
C	lawn in the middle of the square as useable space

B

A-B the patio with cut Box-tree and Rhododenron

Festival Hall of Weissach

Landscape: relais Landschaftsarchitekten
Architect: Peter W. Schmidt Architekt BDA
Location: Weissach, Germany
Client: Municipal of Weissach
Completion: 2004
Size: 6.500 m^2
Costs: 1.200.000 €
Photographs: Stefan Müller

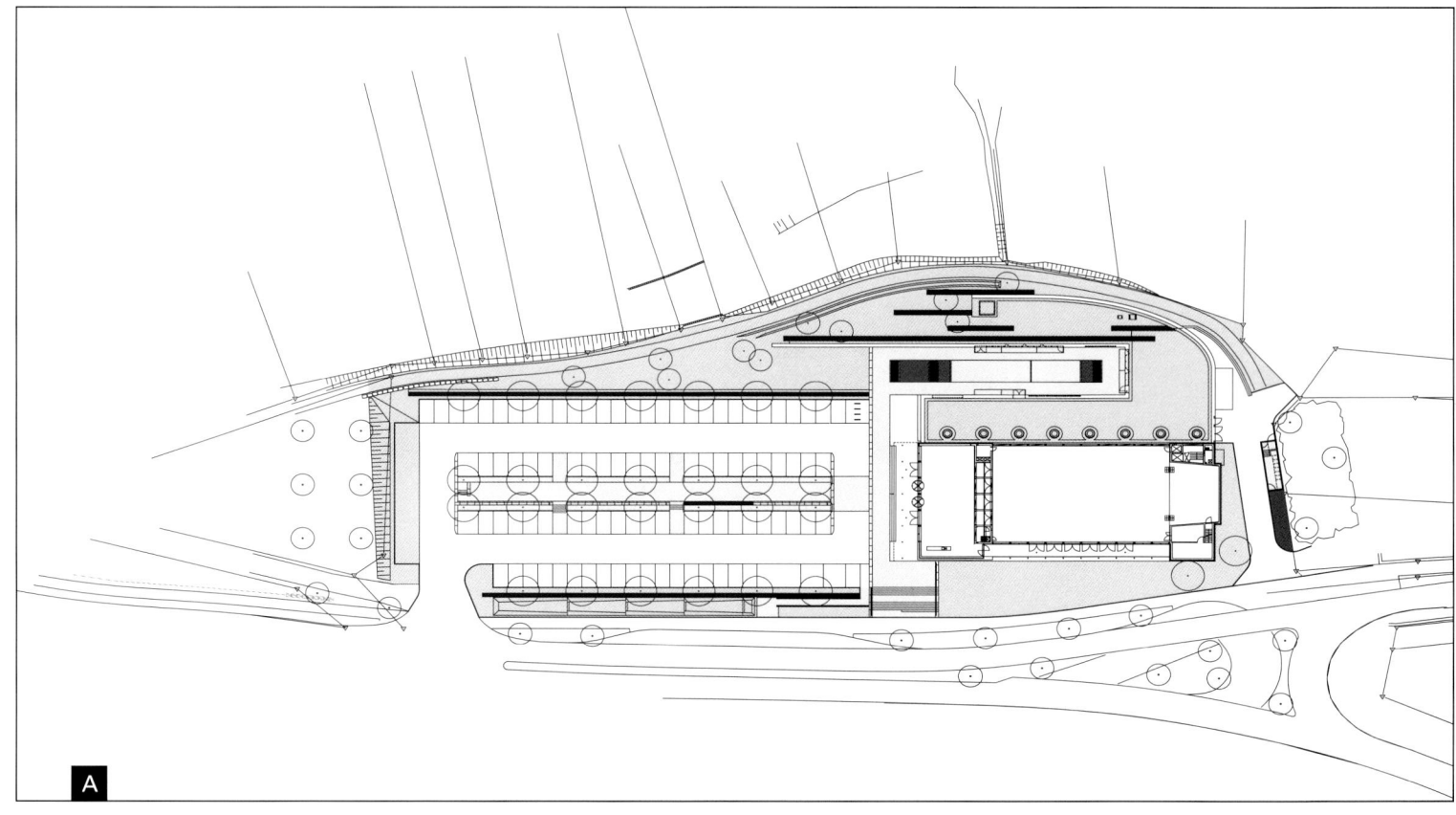

A

The festival hall is located at the entrance of the village and the region is characterizes by its utility landscape of the Strudelbachtals with its fruit plantations. The building offers a representative entrance stair area, entrance terrace and Patio which formulate an appropriate entrée.

The car park area is located in south direction an offer a promenade which is arranged in longitudinal axis of this car park to guides the visitor to the main entrance of the festival hall. A clear slope situation marks the topographical relief with a level difference of 8 m from northeast to south west. The area is developed by the terraced terrain.

Support walls follow the course of the heights lines and connect very sensitive the festival hall with the existing topography. Beech hedges adorn the walls as a "green skin" and offer a harmony relation to the scenic environment of fruit plantations and gardens.

A	master plan
B-C	a promenade which guides to the main entrance of the hall

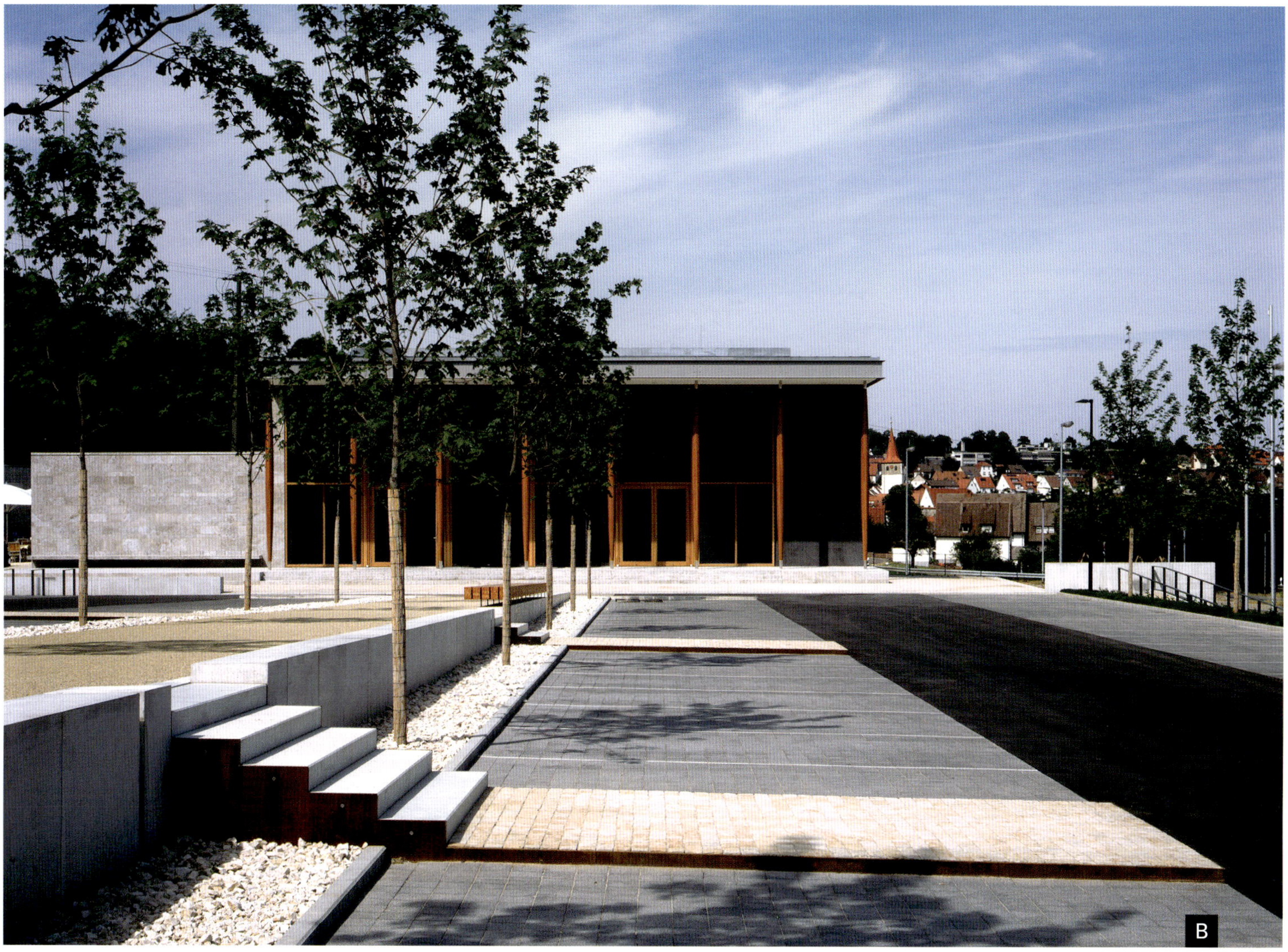

B

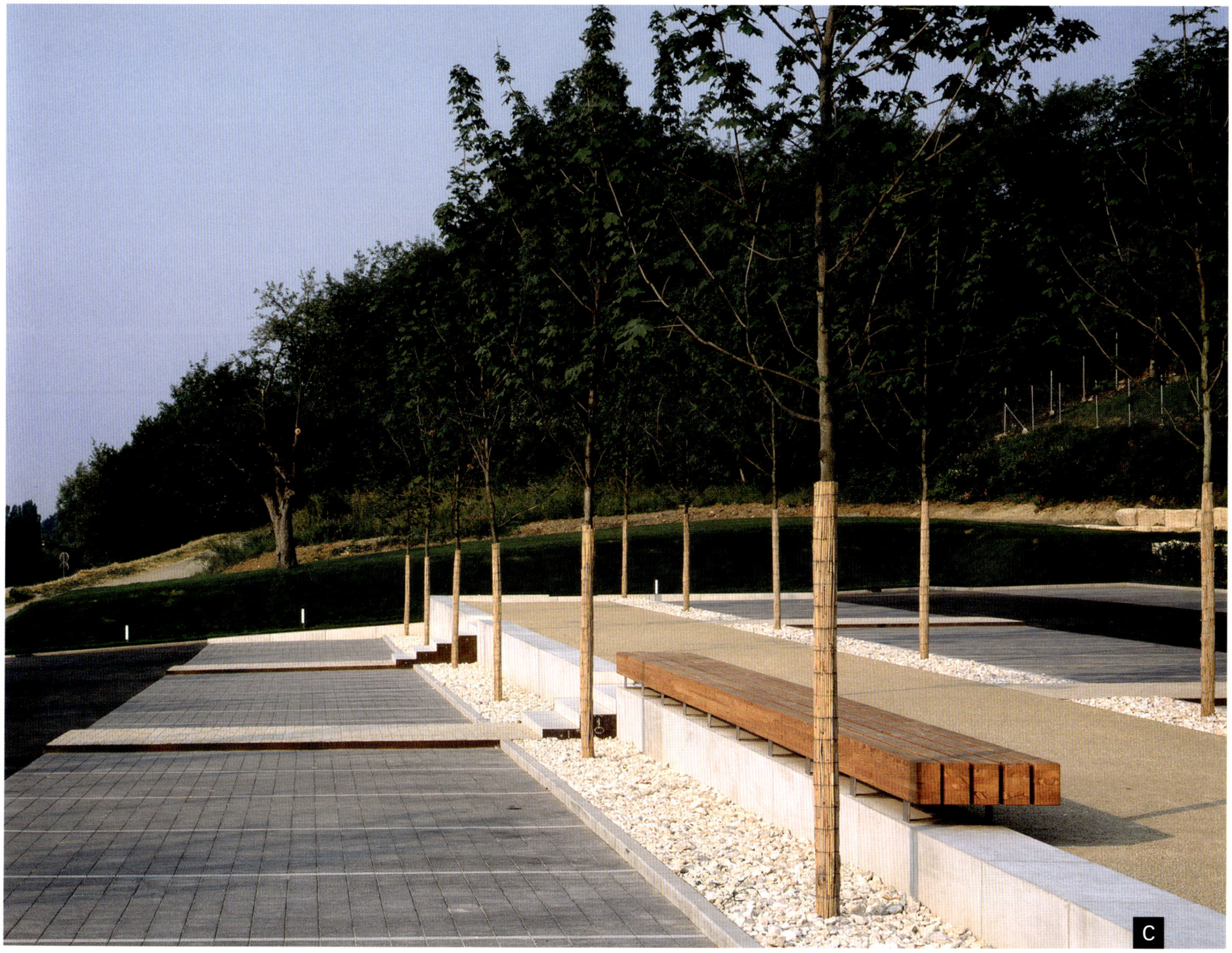

C

A

STRUDELBACH

B

A ribbons of hedges on the roof

B stair to the terrace of the main entrance

C the rain water seep away in hollows

B

A the Platanus tree stands irregular all over the square in polygonal concrete elements

B view over the square and the embed tram rails

Tessinerplatz

Landscape:	KuhnTruninger Landschaftsarchitekten
Location:	Zürich, Switzerland
Client:	Civil Engineering Departement Zürich
Completion:	2006
Size:	7.500 m^2
Costs:	ca. 1.800.000 sFr (1.200.000 €)
Photographs:	KuhnTruninger Landschaftsarchitekten

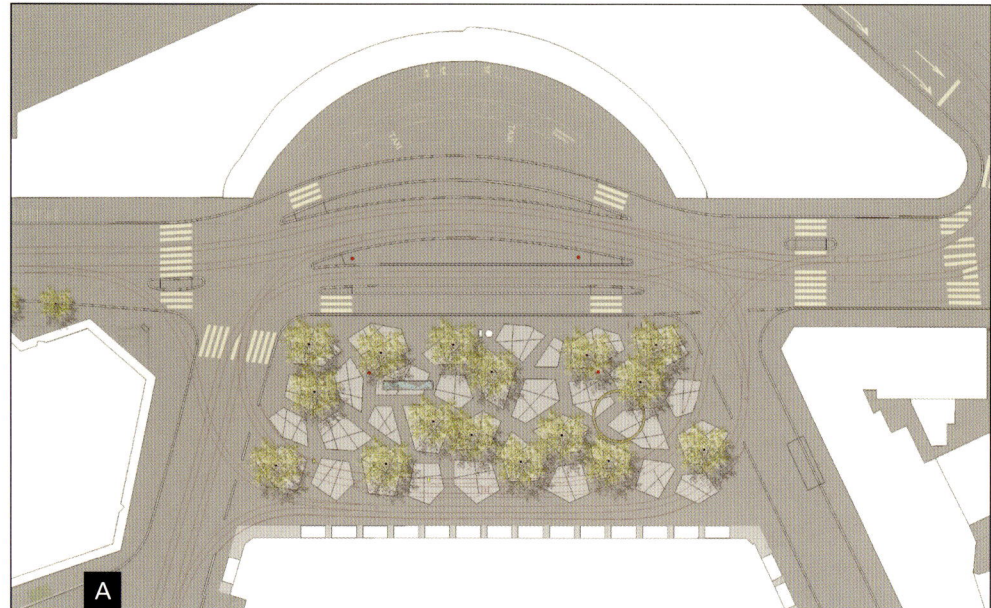

A

For many tourists and foreign workers was the train station „Enge" the "gate to the south", here began the journey back to the homeland or in vacation. At the opposite it was the place of arrivals from the south. The function as a long-distance railway station has change in the meantime to a regional traffic junction with a daily frequency of 45'000 persons.

The reorganization and redesign of the Tessiner Square clarified in the first and important measure the situation of the urban space. The railway station "Enge" was built around 1926/27 by the brothers Pfister. The building was built in a half moon shape to create a forecourt as entrance ensemble between the train station building and the parallel crossing main street "Seestrasse". Just back in the 80th's the building line was set back in the favour for the arising traffic. The forecourt of the train station becomes bigger but the urban situation was still unsolved. Over the last decades a provisional design became manifested.

Today a roof of trees will forms the new opposite of the train station and clarifies the spatial situation of the existing free urban space. The square surface is covered with a uniform pavement which ensures the biggest conductivity. A "carpet" of oversize and irregular slaps made by upgraded monolithic concrete is playing with the picture of the typical "Tessiner Garten Slaps". The surfaces of the concrete slaps are assembled by black and white components which follow the structure of gneiss. The Platanus tree (Platanus acerifolia), a very familiar tree in Zurich, will over span the square in 5 meters heights and creating a roof of trees.

Two large single elements occupied the square very carefully and support simplicity and clarity of the square design. A monolithic wells made by granite from Cevio Maggia Valley was designed by Horst Bohnet in cooperation with the sculptors association. The kind of stone and the design of the well are reflecting the typical region of Tessin. A second element is a wood ring made by Oregon pine with a diameter of 8 meters. The ring invite as rest and common area pedestrian and inhabitants.

A site plan

B the square out of pedestrian view

A

B

A future view with the roof of trees

B pattern of polygonal slaps and asphalt surface

C-D the wooden bench in front of the facade invite pedestrians to relax

A

A view to the new square and new building
B view to the harbour tram and the Schwedler Lake
C new building and new square in context to the historical
 urban structure

Heinz Raspe Plaza

Landscape:	B.A.E.R. Becsei-Hackenbracht
Location:	Frankfurt on Main, Germany
Client:	Hafen Frankfurt
Completion:	2005
Size:	3600 m^2
Costs:	1.480.000 €
Photographs:	Stephan Becsei, Christine Hackenbracht

Lindleystraße

Pumpenhaus

Netzstation

Platanenhain

Vorhaltefläche Café

Hafenbahn

Uferweg - Fortführung auf den Nachbargrundstücken

Nordbecken

A

The Heinz-Raspe-Platz is situated in the eastern part of Frankfurt on Main at the riverside, near to the East Harbour called 'Osthafen'.

The East Harbour, has been developed over the past years into a modern goods logistics centre on the basis for the "Harbour 2000+" concept. In 2005, approximately 1,800 ships docked and set off from here.

According to the reorganisation of the Frankfurt Harbour Management Company (HFM)a new office-building was planned in 'Lindleystraße', as well as a parking garage and the 'Kontorhaus', which offers production and display areas, along with offices and stores.

The open space between the office building of HFM and the parking garage has become an attractive plaza with trees and seats for relaxing and taking breath during the lunch-time. Events like the 1.Harbour Festival in 2006 took place on the 'Heinz-Raspe-Platz'.

The design and form of that public space has structurally been determined by the architecture of the HFM office building. The pattern of the prefabricated concrete floor covering and the brick lining refers to the façade and column intervals. Covered with 9 platanus trees a square ground, situated in the middle of the open space, offers shady seats.

At night the 'Heinz-Raspe-Platz' is illuminated by more than 30 upright lights and 20 floor lights, which accentuates that public space and makes it visible to the south-side of the Main

A	site plan
B	people from surrounding use the square as common area
C	the raster of the square follow the structure of the building facade

B

C

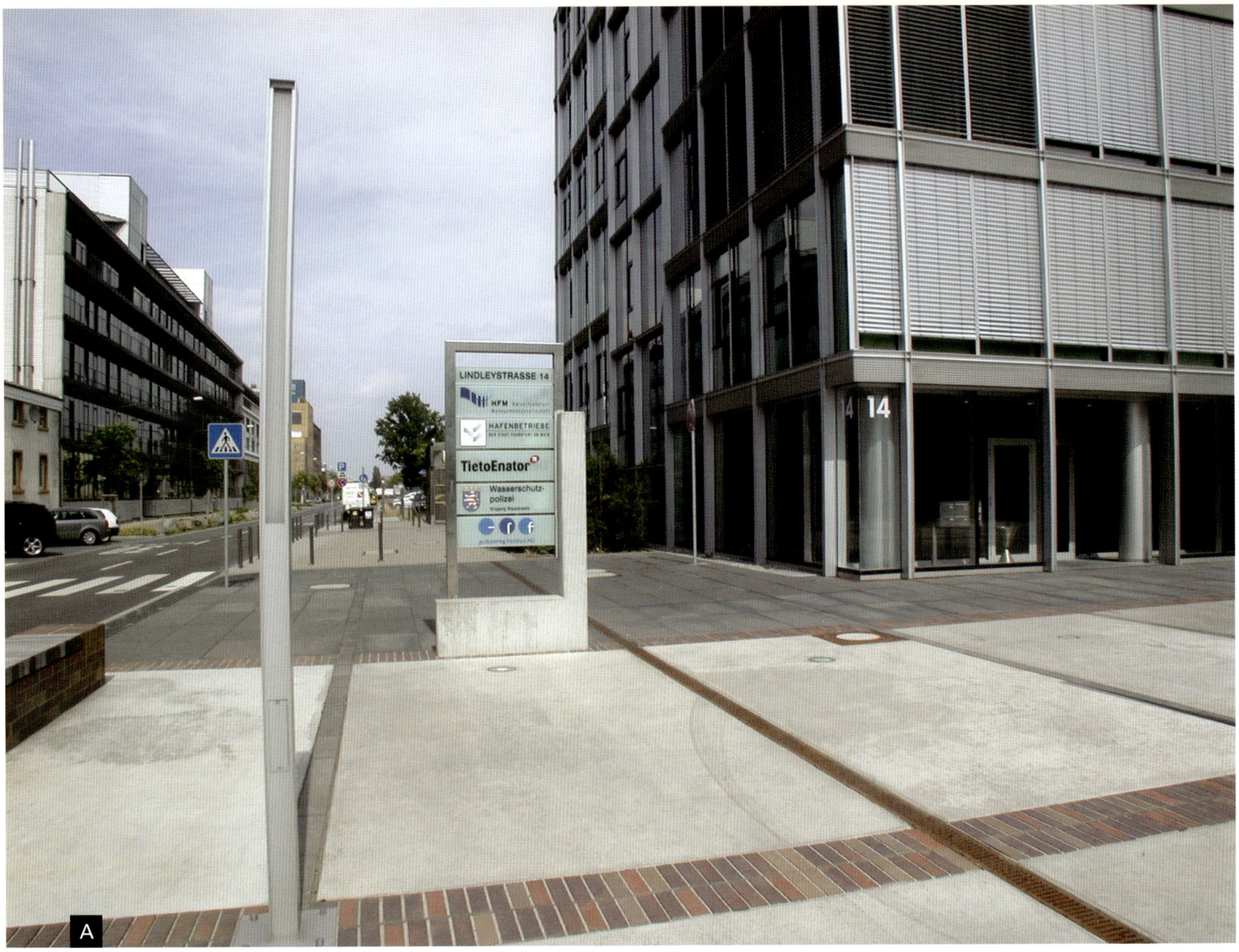
LINDLEYSTRASSE 14
HFM
HAFENBETRIEBE
TietoEnator
Wasserschutz-
polizei
14

A

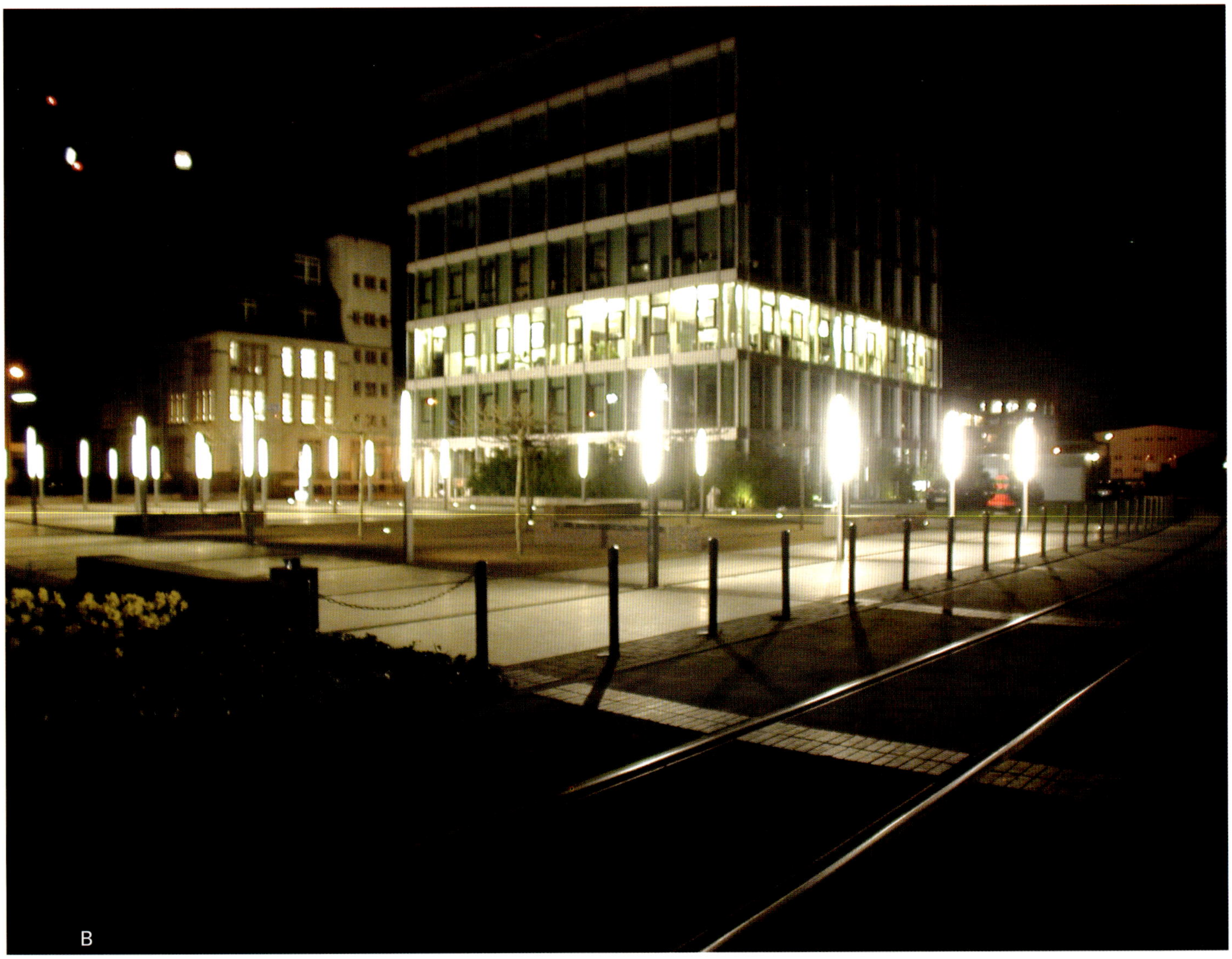

B

C

A the concrete areas are divided by Basalt
  stones and brink stones

B illuminated Heinz Raspe Plaza

C view to south over the square

A

A transition space between the commercial buildings
and the residential area
B inner residential square

Alcântara Rio

Landscape:	PROAP, Lda.
Location:	Alcântara, Lisbon, Portugal
Client:	Grupo Obriverca, Somague PMG
Completion:	2003
Size:	11.706 m^2
Costs:	670.000 €
Photographs:	Leonardo Finotti

A

The conversion of the former União Fontaínhas Factory (ALCÂNTARA-RIO, S.A.) is part of a global urban solution which establishes diversified outdoor spaces along the main avenue (Av. de Ceuta). These spaces are conceptually united with the definition of an exclusively pedestrian area, which forms a series of inner block situations, protected from the external aggressiveness and simultaneously open to the surroundings.

The diversity of the outdoor space is based on two urban solutions limited by the street with more intense circulation (Rua Fradesso da Silveira and Av. de Ceuta) and that can be distinguished in inner leisure areas and peripheral circulation areas. The squares defined by the new buildings create more reserved spaces, intentionally defined as higher affluence areas. The intention of the squares is to share corresponding residential use with the buildings. The outdoor circulation area is, on the other hand, intimately related to pedestrian flows that cross the spaces and the services that are offered by commercial and office buildings, thus assuming the public character of a pedestrian street.

These two typologies are separated by a change of level, which is solved with, gentle gradient, pedestrian ramps that relate with the tilted, metal and vegetation, planes. The metal – corten steel – arises from an agreement with the architectural design, reinstating the former industrial image. A decisive contribute to this image is the landscape integration of the former factory chimney.

The underground ventilation system is integrated in the tilted sheets of orange metal, finely perforated to allow airing.

A master plan

B night view with the old chimney of the Ancient
Factory União das Fontainhas

A

B

A new garden area with an old element / memory of the Ancient Factory União das Fontaínhas

B grass shapes over underground parking slab, with trees and shrubs. White concrete modular benches

A

B

C

D

A	border area between residential and commercial spaces
B	emergency access to the inner squares
C	night view of an inner square
D	corten Steel slopes with underground ventilation

A

A steel staircase along a architectural concrete wall
B steel staircase

Trumpf-Sachsen

Landscape:	BÜRO KIEFER
Architect:	Barkow Leibinger Architekten Berlin
Location:	Neukirch, Germany
Client:	Trumpf Sachsen GmbH
Completion:	2006
Size:	8.000 m^2
Costs:	500.000 €
Photographs:	Hanns Joosten

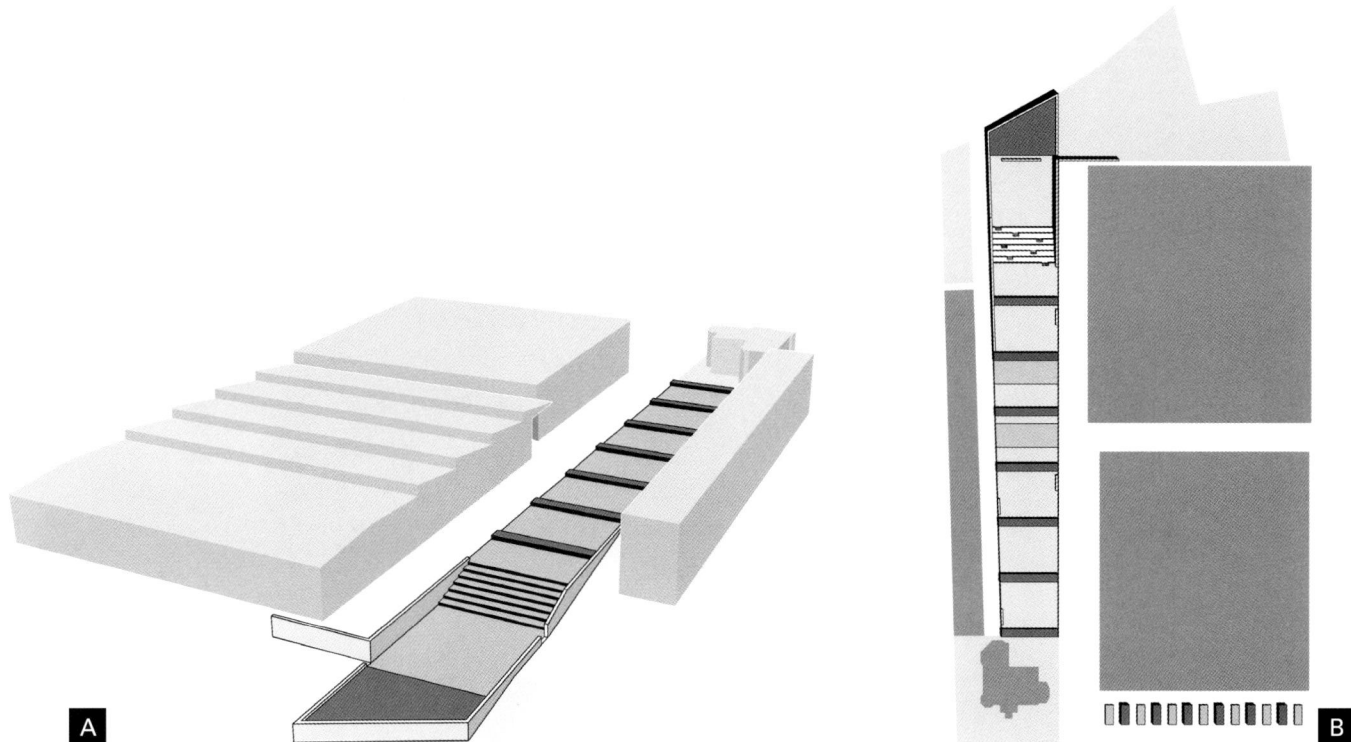

A company producing precision tools in Saxony; the outdoor areas were redesigned as part of the production plant extension programs. The central area in the design is the so-called landscape corridor, built within the open landscape of the surrounding area. The corridor links the two flanks of the production site, creates areas in which employees but also transport vehicles, can move around, links the car park and the employee's garden. Production procedures make it sensible to use clear articulation into strips as a design principle. At the same time, steps were envisaged because of the height differences. The company's product range meant that metal was predestined to be a theme in the architecture and in the outdoor space. It becomes the key material in the steps area. Water-polished stainless steel in the flight of steps, manufactured with individually developed detail, forms a counterpart to the façade of the new buildings.

The material's clear form and cool aura set off the coarse basalt gravel path coverings and paving and also the planting with box, blue lavender and white shrub roses. The clear definition of the site as a commercial location weights the design less towards atmosphere and more towards manageability – and thus creates that very quality. In this concept, steel in the form of the edge bands, staircase strings and hand rails, takes on the function of threads in a network of fine lines into which fittings and design elements can be hung. Here the charm lies in playing with serial qualities and arrangement. Consistent use of a material canon representing the tool firm itself, perfected in detail and composed to create an overall picture from everyday materials: reduced, ergonomic and striking.

C

A axonometrical view

B site plan

C factory garden

A steel staircase

B main axe through factory area

C front garden

A

B

C

A

B

A view into the central park
B playground

Living and Working in Park City

Landscape:	Rainer Schmidt Landschaftsarchitekten
Architect:	Andre Perret
Location:	Munich Schwabing, Germany
Client:	City Tec Munich
Completion:	2002
Size:	4,2 ha
Costs:	3.000.000 €
Photographs:	Steffen Grau, Michael Heinrich

A

Subjects gardens as heart pieces of the central park area

The central public green area has as a representative park a high identification valued. The central park will give the new arising district an own character also on the level of landscape design. Next to the recovery function for the residents, the park is also a communication and stay area for the employees of the neighbor business zones.

On a length of ca. 600 m and a width of ca. 70 m the park unit organizes itself into a sequence of tree areas and free meadow areas. Interspersed into these extensive areas are thematic designed gardens which are equipped with topographical and garden elements as well as game arrangements.

These gardens show as an abstracted spoof the different landscapes between Munich and the Alps which are well visible from the high buildings by good weather. They follow along one ´red ribbon` into the total area, offer however a new scale with its finely divided structure. Cross ways with single trees are organizing the park landscape and they are the connection to the residential areas.

B

A master plan

B view along the main axis

A

B

A field garden

B rock lake garden

C rock and boulders garden

A atrium
B atrium, a unique mixture of materials

Federal Environmental Agency - Nature in Motion

Landscape:	ST raum a. landcape architecture
Architect:	sauerbruch hutton architekten
Location:	Dessau, Germany
Client:	Superior Finance Directorate Magdeburg
Completion:	2006
Size:	2 ha
Costs:	1.800.000 €
Photographs:	Marcus Bredt

The new Federal Environmental Agency building in the form of a loop reveals imaginative spaces in the inner and outer areas. Ecological requirements, such as the use of environmentally friendly materials, and special building techniques played a major role in planning of buildings and open spaces. The open space elements are symbolised as artifical "biocells" which are presented along the promenade in varying themes: the island of dead trees, rocky roots, yew strudel, wind / weather stones and Benje's snakes. The covered inner courtyard appears as an artificial landscape with water, reflection and texture areas as well as various exotic shrubs. A memorable design of the elements, whose unique materiality and specific selection of plants create an area that is conquered and patinated by nature and enriches the Dessau-Wörlitz garden realm.

B

A master plan

B plaza between main entrance and cafeteria

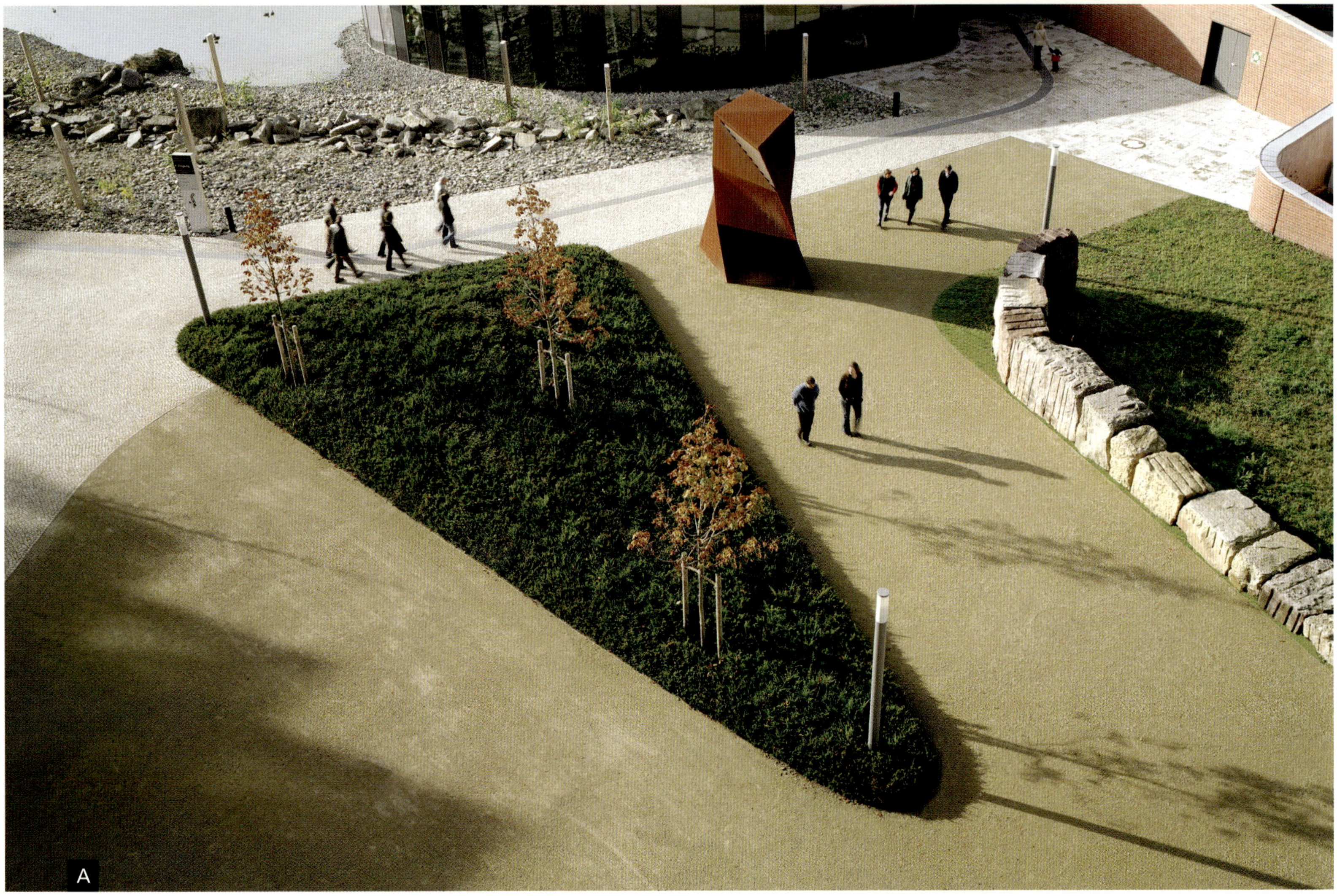
A

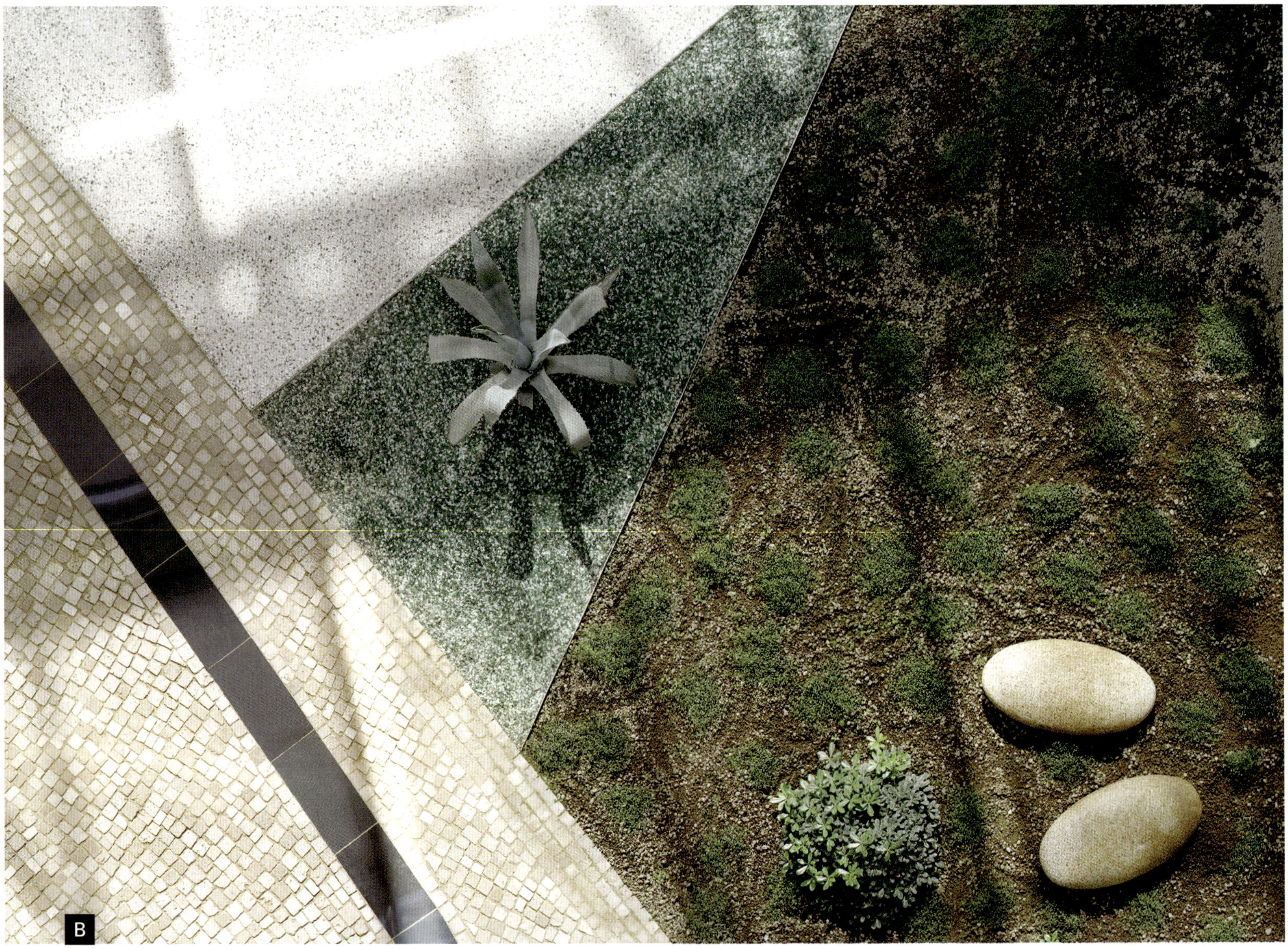
B

A forecourt between main entrance and canteen

B atrium, glass surfaces and stone ellipses

C stacked wood hedge

D corten steel air exchange tower

A

B

A retentionbassin with rainwater
B waterfall to aerate the Retentionsbassin
C fountain with rainwater, from a subterraneous Cistern

Innovations Centre Getrag Company

Landscape:	Landschaft Drei, Michael F. Heintze
Architect:	Neugebauer & Rösch
Location:	Untergruppenbach near Heilbronn, Germany
Client:	GETRAG Corporate Group
Completion:	2004
Size:	5.4 ha
Costs:	3,250.000 €
Photographs:	Michael F. Heintze

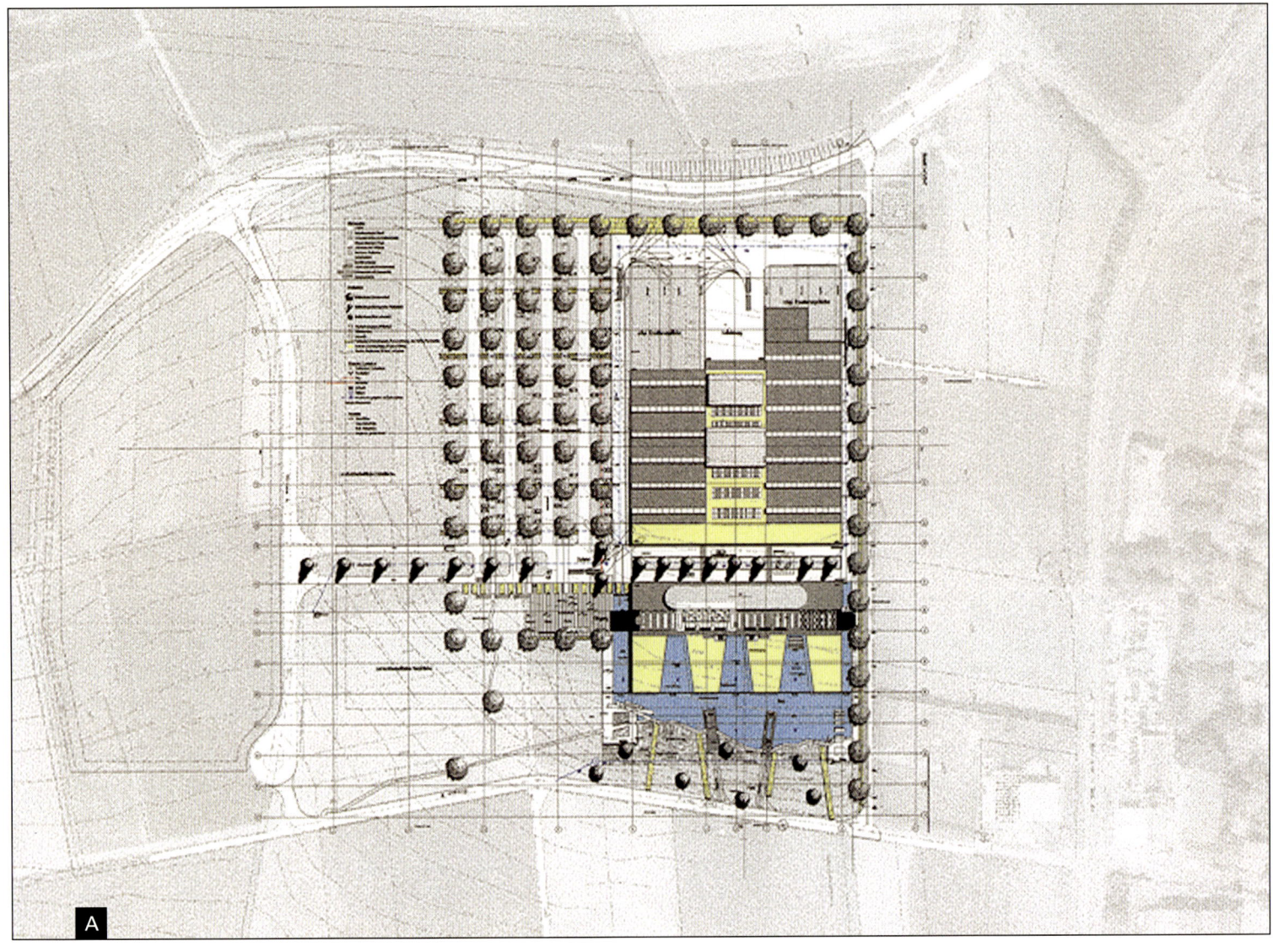

Development planning,
Excavation,
Rainwater management,
Planting vegetation of internal space
Ext. planting vegetation of housetops
Designing of undeveloped areas

The Innovation Center with its workshops, offices, cafeteria, schooling and conference building
is a building for research and progression. The big building is infixed in the landscape with very
different means.

The correlations between inside and outside are multifaceted!
Water elements and accurately designed appurtenant structures encourage the integration
into the nature and increase the quality of employments.

B

A master plan

B infiltration of surfacewater from the parking area

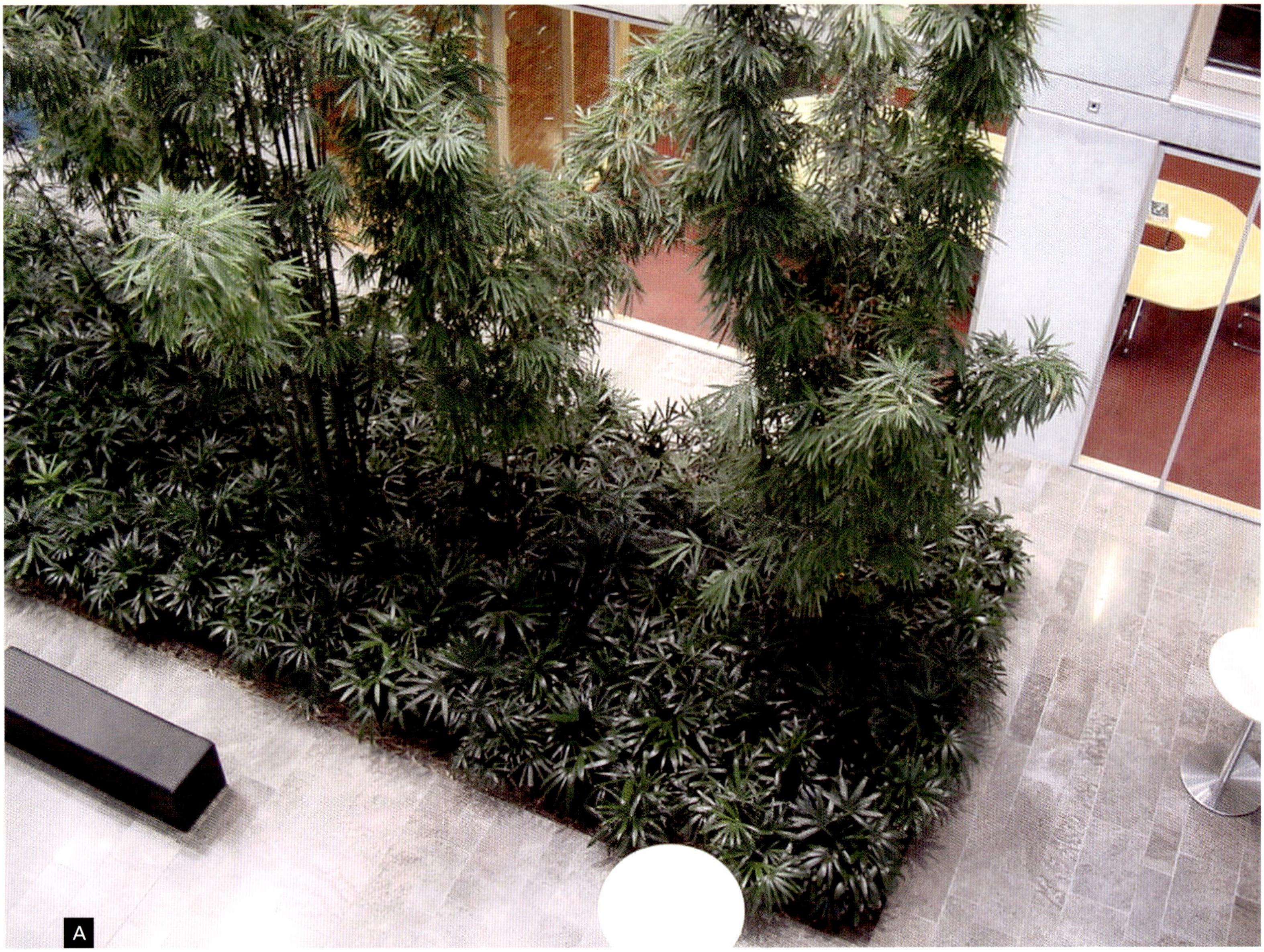
A

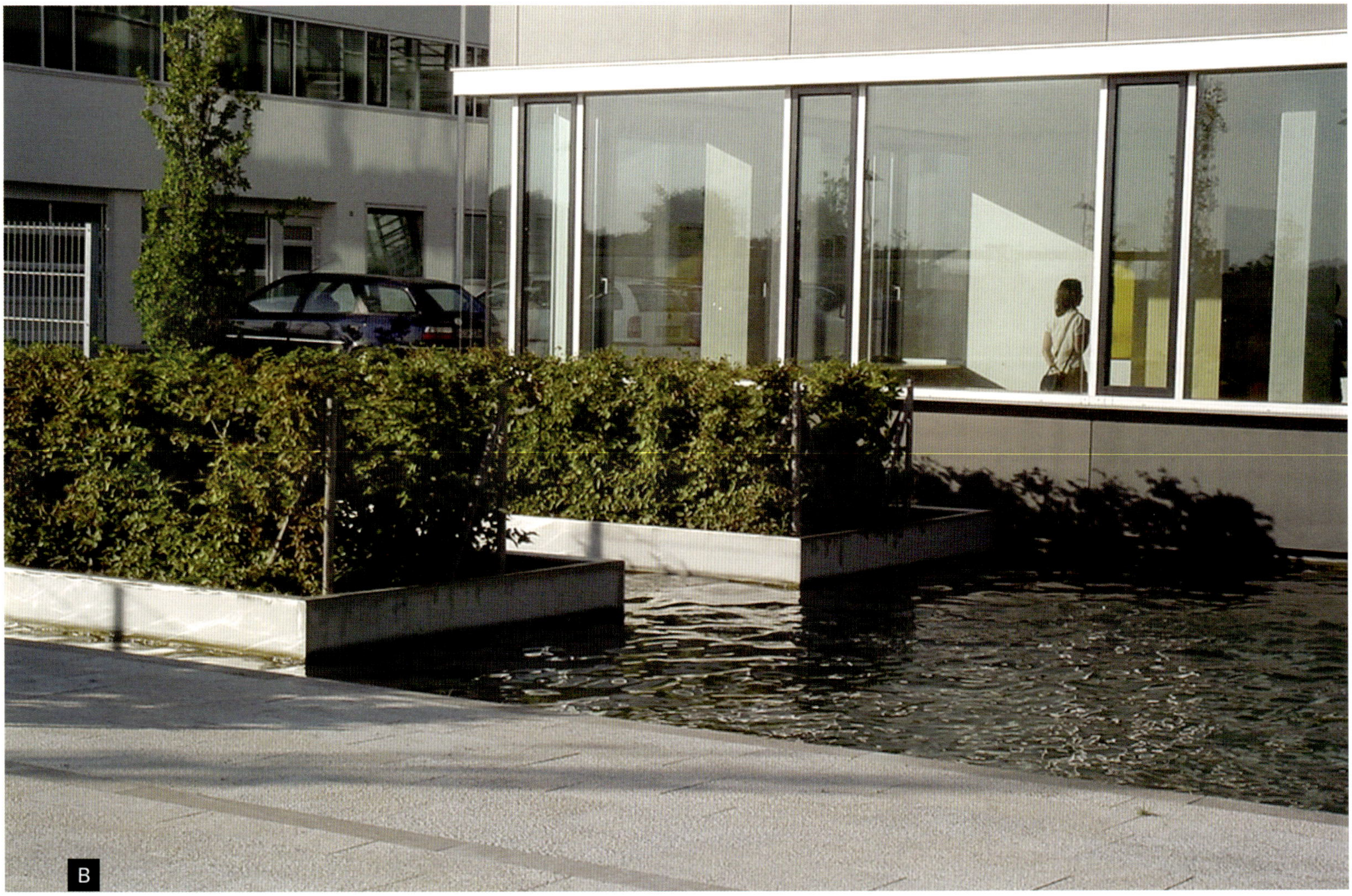
B

C

A interior planting with bamboo

B swimming hedges

C retentionbassin with waterfalls

B

A the sofa shaped objects and the trees continue straight
  through the indoor space in the atrium

B looking towards the atrium from the new planted meadow
  with birch trees which interacting with the sculptural objects

Common Ground

Landscape:	Monika Gora
Location:	Umeå, Sweden
Client:	Västerbotten County Council
Completion:	2002
Size:	4746 m^2
Costs:	150.000 €
Photographs:	Florian Kynman, Jan Lindmark

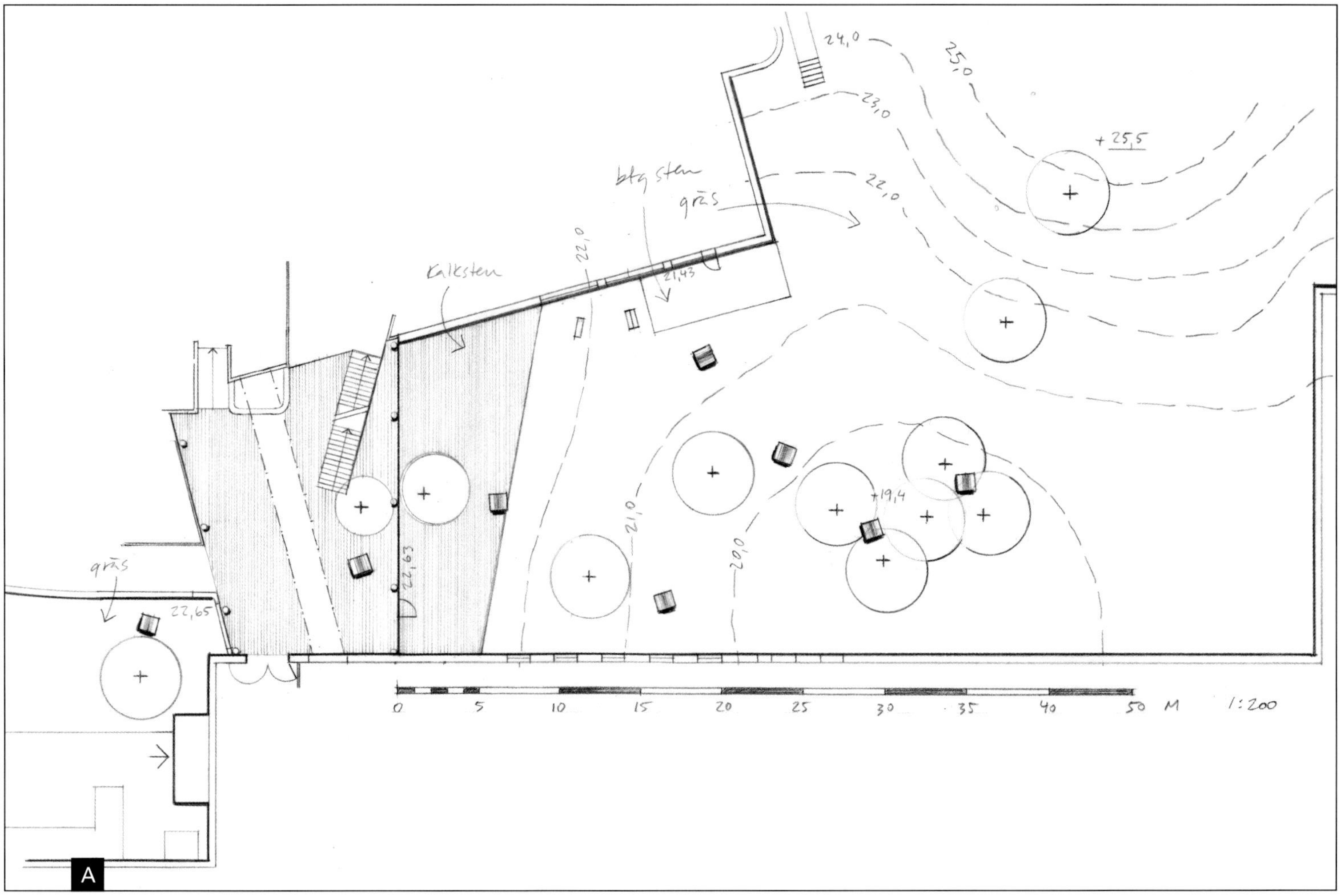

A

landscape, sculpture, light

Sculpture commission that resulted in landscaping of a larger area. The landscape continues right through a hall with glass walls. The continuity is enhanced by scattered trees, sculptures that follow the modelling of the ground. One of the trees is inside the hall and almost touches the closest tree outside. The other trees are spread in small clusters on the meadows outside. The sculptures are all the same shape, but of two different materials; one is of black diabase, the rest of magenta pigmented polyester reinforced with glass fibre in varying colour saturation. The shape of a heart or a sofa or a flower..... and lighted by fluorescent lamps. The stone floor in the hall also continues on the terrace outside. Everything continues.

The title Common Ground refers to - the ground as the common land, an unifying platform for life in different shapes.

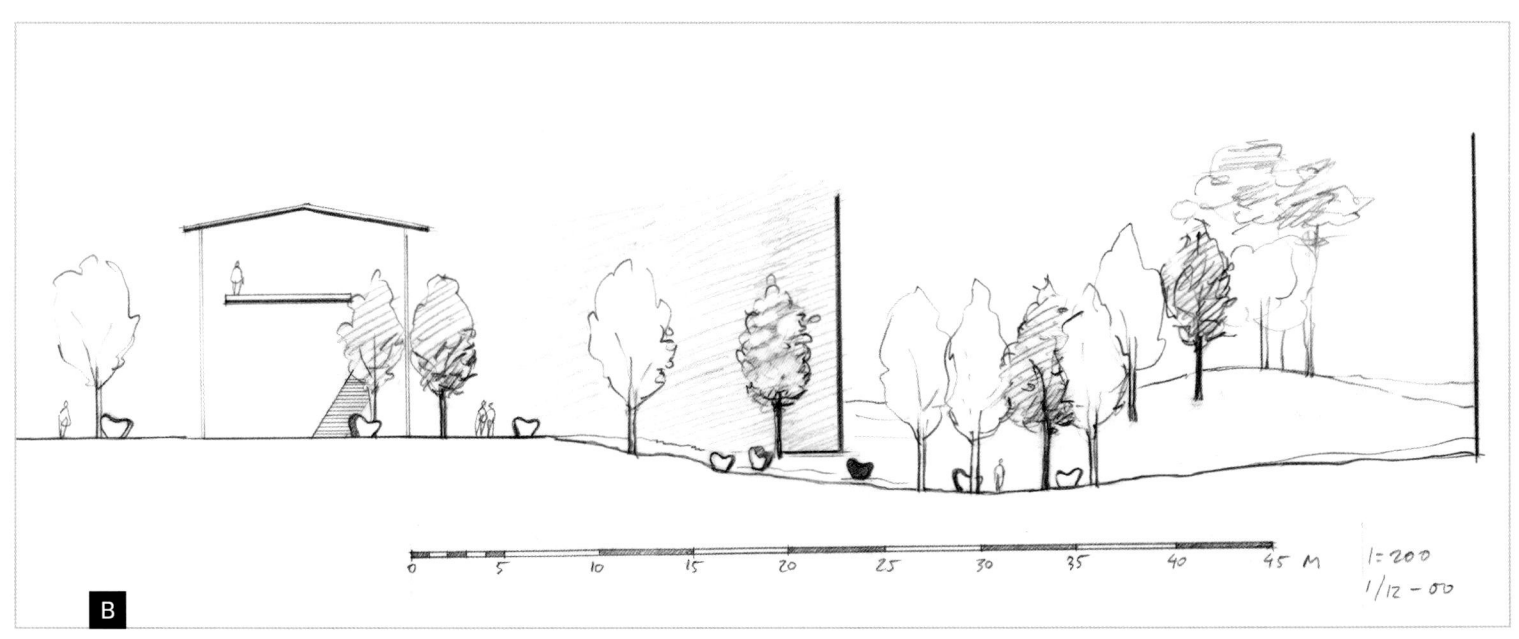

B

C

A master plan

B section

C the interior space of the atrium, in the background a Podocarpus tree

A

B

C

D

A view from the terrace right outside the Atrium

B the design with the soft rolling landscape and high grass is unique in the hospital area of Umeå

C the lightning design attract especially in wintertime when it is dark most of the daytime in Umeå, located far north in Europe

D the reflections multiply the glowing images

A

B

A the campeon seen from the parkside
B roofed pathway to the tram platform
C cafeteria with terrace and entrance to the water

Headquarter Infineon Campeon

Landscape:	Gnüchtel – Triebswetter Landscape architects
Architect:	tec architects Los Angeles + Maier Neuberger Partner Munich
Location:	Munich-Unterhaching, Germany
Client:	MoTo Objekt Campeon GmbH & Co. KG
Completion:	2006
Size:	ca. 6,2 ha
Costs:	21.000.000 €
Photographs:	Franziska Meyer, Tobias Granetzny

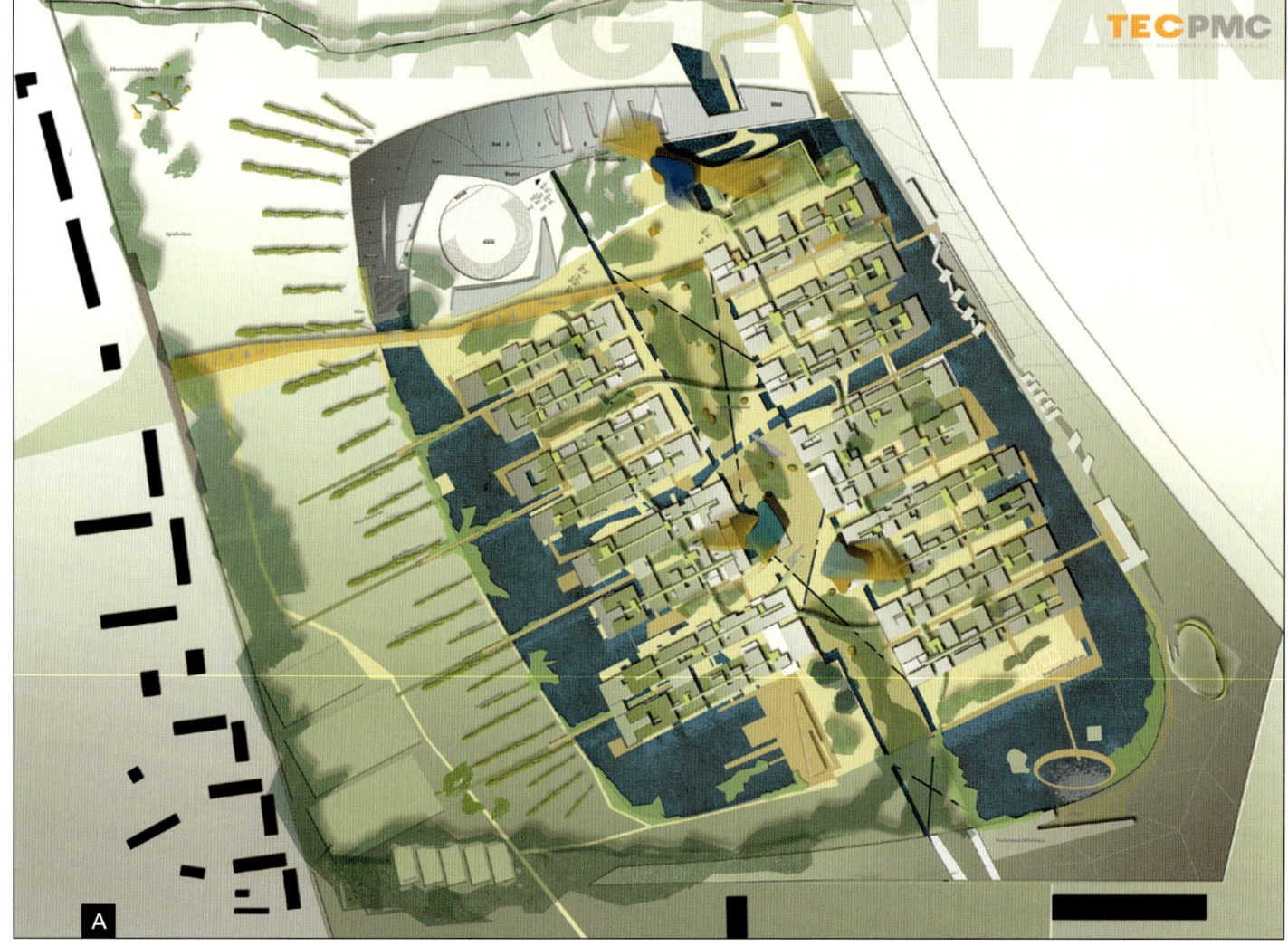

Modular architecture in small units in a flowing nuanced and elaborated landscape with a central park and a ring of water. The campus subdivides into the actual office complex and a naturalistically designed people's park being the direct extension of the existing Unterhachinger Sports Park. This creates one continuous park landscape open to the public in the south of Munich. An earth embankment blocks off the landscape from the motorway and provides a noise barrier.

A U-shaped pond encloses the modular buildings of the Campeon, bordered by a waterside promenade and crossed by footbridges that provide access to the people's park. Like a heart, the office area has two halves, each with modules and interstitial spaces oriented in an east-west direction. In the middle, a spacious green runs through the grounds from north to south.

The ring-shaped, 6.8-hectare Campeon pond improves the microclimate and serves as a retention and seepage basin for the rainwater coming from the building roofs. Tastefully laid out, the pond is fed by rainwater and snow. In order to keep water quality high, the water is changed completely once a year. The planners do this by introducing small quantities of groundwater besides the rainwater from May to September and directing the pond's water through reed filtering tanks – forming a natural purification plant – during this time.

B

C

A master plan

B silent place for recreation in front of the water

C inflow of water

A footbridge to the parkside

B sunked garden - way to the tram platform

C example for an edge at the campus side

D one of the many footbridges to the park

A

B

A the courtyard shows different views
B the ornamental basic structure can find in all elements of
  the courtyard design
C already 2 month after the completion the structure of the
  plants are visible

Swiss Life

Landscape:	planivers Landschaftsarchitekten
Artist:	Jürg Moser
Location:	Zurich, Switzerland
Client:	Pension Institute Swiss Life Zurich
Completion:	2006
Size:	1200 m^2
Costs:	1.000.000 SFr
Photographs:	Ralph Feiner

Foyer

Personalrestaurant

A

During the current total renewal of the Swiss Life headquarters in Zurich, the courtyard also received a timely new design. The project designers are Jürg Moser and the planivers landscape architects.

The current reorganisation considers manifold claims and expectations at the courtyard. On the one hand the courtyard will be available for customers and visitor of the Swiss Life out of the entrance hall to an optical eye-catcher, on the other hand it should be available as an outside zone for the employees of the employee's restaurant in the summer months. Thereto the functional requests of the goods transfer which insert themselves inconspicuously into this scenario.

From building detached courtyard area defines an independent room. By means of shape and differentiation of the surface areas and green areas, the most different requests as well as grass planting, traffic ability and ride ability has been brought optically together. With the new formation, the courtyard receives an own identity that itself stand out against the geometrically-architectural structure of the surrounding facade.

Similar like a carpet is the polished poured asphalt patterned with iron ribbon. In the same shaping are formulated the marked steel hollow wall and the footpath made by limestone concrete. According to view angle, the playful pattern can produce picture impressions in most different ways.

The plant fields which lay like belts in the landscape are planted like a meadow with circa 4'500 enduring flowers onions, shrubs and grasses. In the spring are dominate blue blooming onion plants. The summer is characterizes with orange and red colours. In the autumn, the gold yellow, smelling foliage of the ginger bread trees and the straw yellow of grasses illuminate in the clear autumn air. The changing colors and spatial impressions make the seasons intensively tangibly.

A site plan

B a variation of the basic structure lay between the China-reed (Miscanthus sinensis)

A

B

A the courtyard is a relaxing space

B nature and architecture in change

C colorful bands of plants in different color

A

B

C

A new plant mulberry trees in front of the older existing trees
B a cross axis connecting the buildings with the city of sciences
C cross streaks made by concrete stay in the contrast to the green lawn and give the courtyard a comfortable atmosphere

Innovation Center for Environment Technology

Landscape:	B. A. E. R. Becsei + Hackenbracht
Location:	Berlin-Adlershof, Germany
Client:	WISTA Management GmbH
Completion:	1999
Size:	14000 m²
Costs:	6.400.000 €
Photographs:	Stephan Becsei, Christine Hackenbracht

The planning of the outside of the "Innovation Centre for Environment Technology" in Berlin-Adlershof was done in relationship to the building concept in close agreement with the planners of building. The five floors high building complex, arranged like a meander, surrounds a 20 metres wide courtyard, which shall be at users' disposal as well as a common place. It is interrupted by an opening axis in North-South direction which lies across to the building axes. Open spaces which border on the 2nd stage of construction should be planned cautious and cost-saving according to their possible alteration. The arrangement of the courtyard adjusts to the references in space and volume which are characterized by the building. The facade is reflected in the water surface and brightens the enormous shady courtyards – depending on the time of day -. Path surfaces are lined with partial pervious surface, e.g. sod pavement, to come up to ecological demands on the one hand, or on the other hand are covered with large slabs to assign calm, unlash outdoor place to the building complex.

The intention of an effective use of environmental resources becomes visible in an intensive green planting of roof expanse, whereby already 8-10% of the coming up rainwater quantity is reduced. The conception of the rainwater-use-unit is based on the protective dealing with the natural drinking water reserve and the relieve of the common waste water network.

A master plan

B view over the courtyard, the concept of the
   organization of longitudinal and cross
   connection to the different buildings is visible

C

D

A bridge over the rainwater drip sink and intake areas

B the 2nd Water basin with overflows in the unconfined area made by prefabricate concrete units

C the water basins offer steps to give the possibility to sit near the water even by less filling

D sit table made by prefabricate concrete units which integrate the existing trees

A climbing stand with blue and white flowering Clematis
B common area with a bed of lavender, columns of wisteria
   flowers and organic shaped sandstone seat objects

Casa Blanca

Landscape:	Dardelet GmbH, Egg ZH, Switzerland
Location:	Uetikon am See, Zurich, Switzerland
Client:	ADT Innova AG, Gossau
Completion:	2003
Size:	20.000 m^2
Costs:	1.500.000 CHF
Photographs:	Jean Dardelet, Oliver Bingler

A

At the right Zurich lakeshore, in Uetikon, at exclusive situation, thirteen multi-family houses for residential property with elevated standard were developed. The 20,000m^2 were built thereby in two stages.

The main emphasis in project engineering was subject to create as much as possible and qualitatively high-quality arrange, usable free space and this under difficult conditions (total covering of underground parking) long-temporally functionally and satisfying.

Differently arranged places, ways and free spaces loosen up the housing development and increase with its high-quality organization the quality of life for that up inhabitant. Developed among other things two attractive park ranges invite to stay and enjoy. Children's game is to be found both on the playground peripheral put on as well as in the generously out-arranged access roads. The environment organization became despite the complicated structural initial position (on underground parkings roof) technically correctly implemented and becomes today still large acceptance and using.

B

A master plan

B all summer round blooming perennial in
yellow and blue

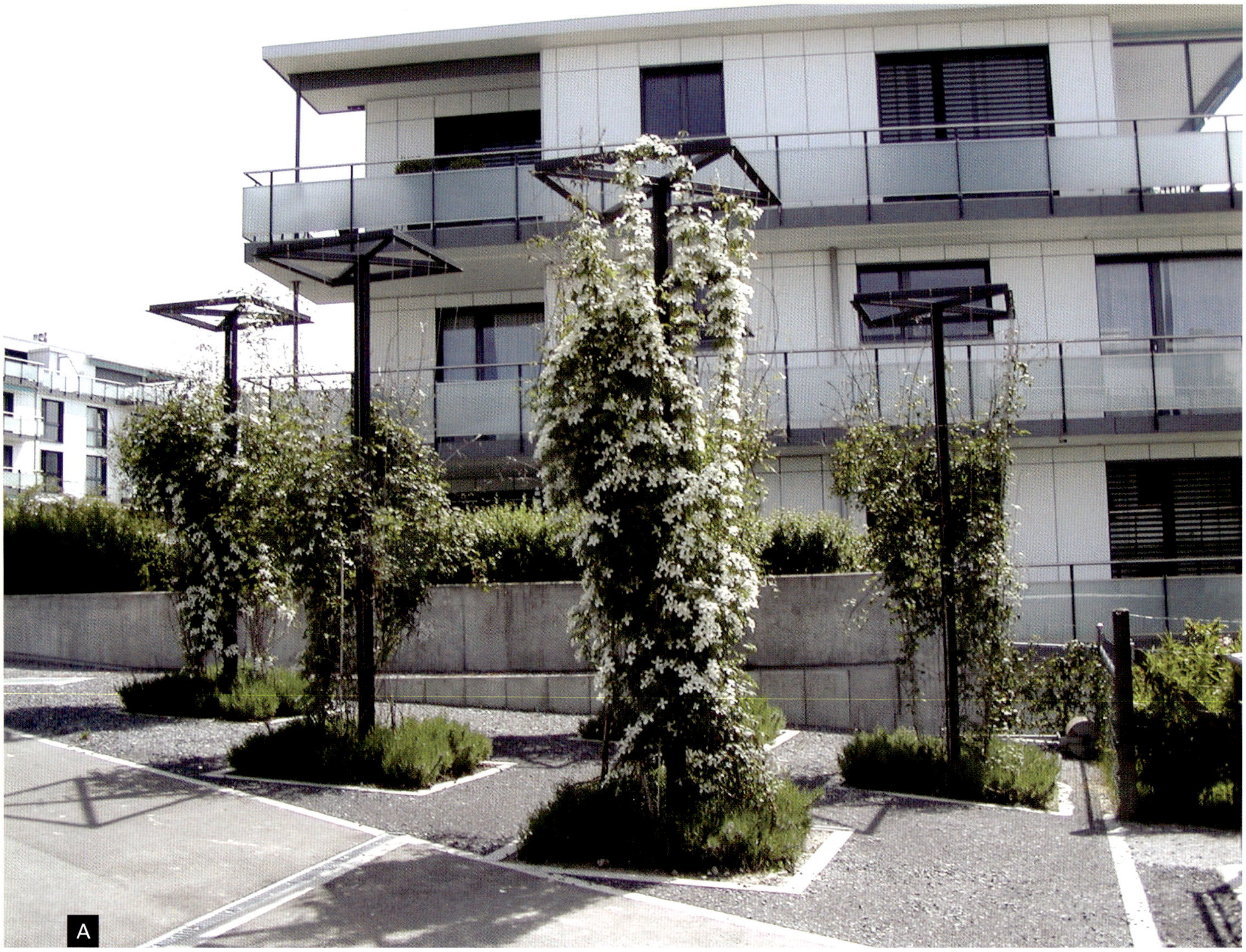
A

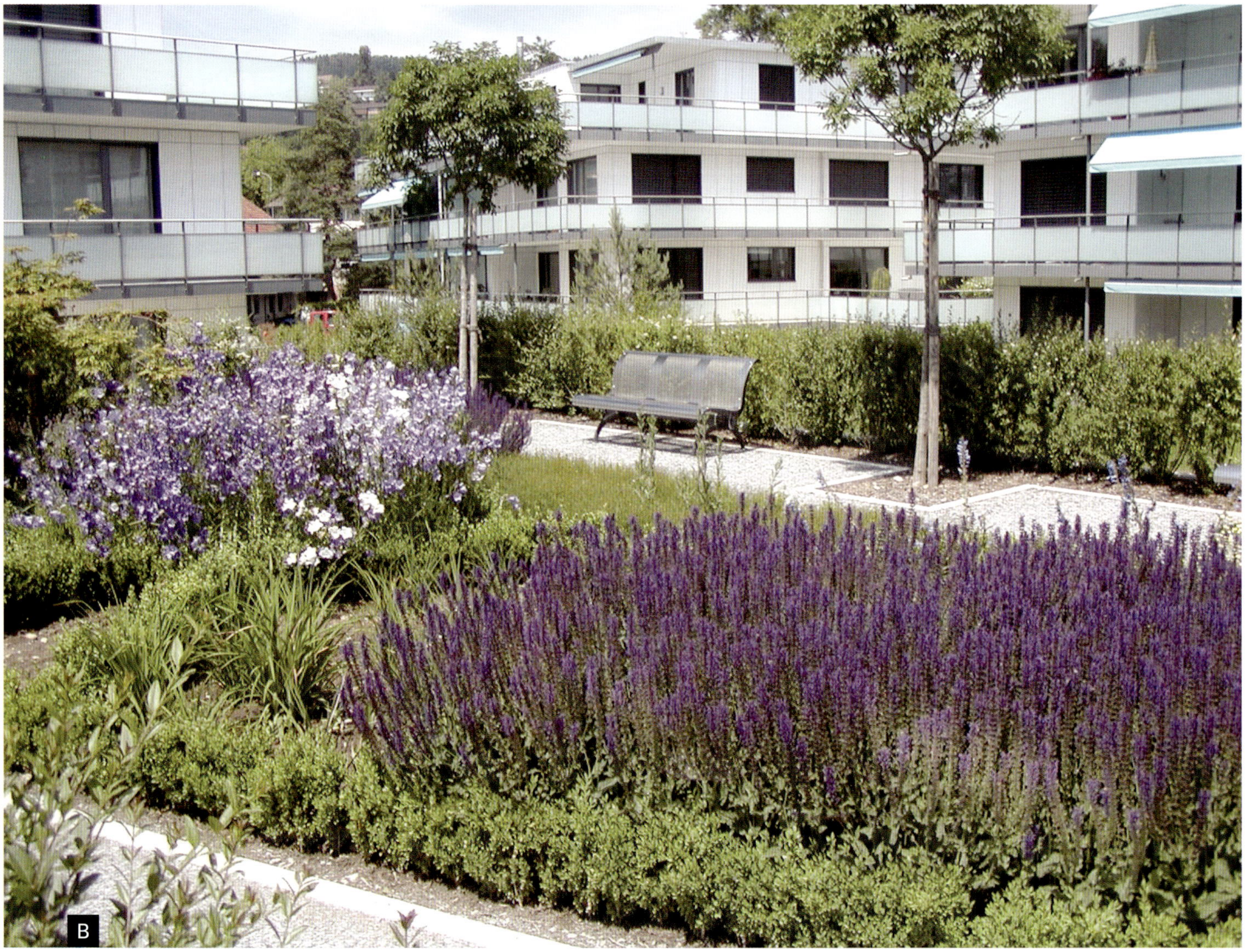
B

C tranquil area in the heart of the residential area

D individual design as a border to a private garden

A foliage scroll with white blossoms in May - June
(blue blossoms during July - September)

B detail of perennial herb planting

C tranquil area in the heart of the residential area

D individual design as a border to a private garden

A view from the upper floor
B the Labyrinth invites children to play

Spreekarree

Landscape:	HÄFNER/JIMENEZ
Design Team:	Thomas Jarosch, Jens Betcke, Carlos Miquel Zurita
Location:	Berlin, Germany
Client:	Meermann Immobilien GmbH
Completion:	2004
Size:	730 m^2
Costs:	160.000 €
Photographs:	Hanns Joosten, Winfried Häfner, Thomas Jarosch

When the developer asked us to present our design for a small 730 square metre courtyard on Friedrichstrasse, a street in the heart of the reunified Berlin, the dice, so to speak, had already been thrown. All of the requirements for the space were well-established and it had been decided that a 20 cm thick layer of earth spread over a concrete slab would be enough to create a garden over an underground car park. Indeed, the slab had already been built.

The courtyard was almost entirely enclosed by buildings and subject to various demands, which had to be met in the design:

• to serve as a break area for residents, visitors and people employed by the surrounding businesses and offices;
• to provide playground space for young children;
• to replace the trees which had been removed in the construction process of the building;
• to limit the bedding on the underground car park to a very small thickness;
• to install a fountain (a demand in all of this developer's projects)
• to maintain an area clear for fire engines.

Finding a solution to all the demands and at the same time creating a pleasant courtyard meant superimposing these many functions and, especially, looking for ways to create a space for the plant roots of more than 20 cm. Mercifully, the car park did not fill the entire space under the parcel, which made it possible to plant trees at the back.

We raised the centre of the courtyard surface with a kerb that rose to 30 cm and filled this space with grass paving which would facilitate the passing of a fire engine in case of emergency. As a decorative but also playful element for the children, we constructed a labyrinth made up of steel jardinières, filled with earth and planted with Carpinus betulus, separated by trees, benches and simple passages. The jardinières are not heavy and provide a maximum volume of earth for the roots. Other jardinières, also of steel, complement the landscaping on the other side of the yard.

The problem of an 80 cm height difference between the buildings was solved with a generous exterior staircase that mediates between the buildings and the courtyard. In addition to providing a place for rest and relaxation, the staircase invites the children to climb and play.

A ground-level fountain that continues the stripe motif and can be easily passed over by fire engines is perhaps the yard's most striking central attraction. In the summer the fountain serves as a recreational element and a paddling pool for children.

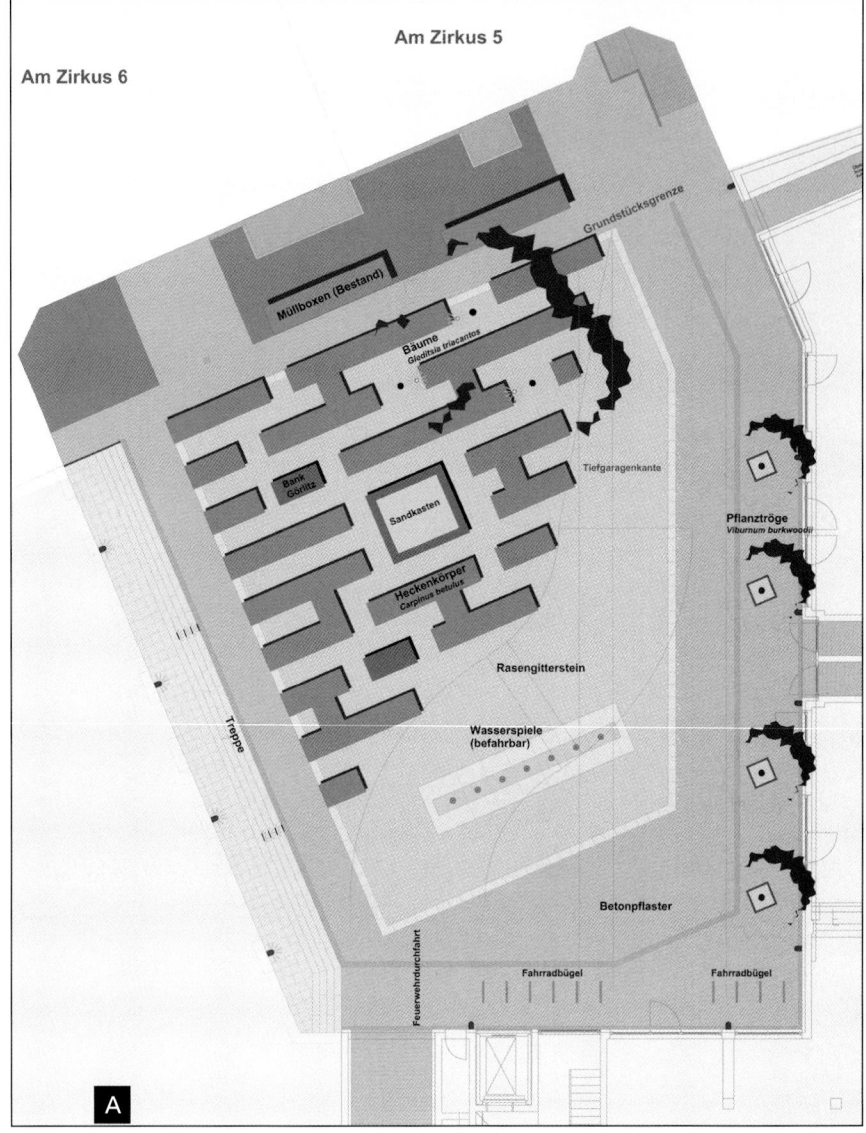

B

A ground floor of the courtyard

B steel panels are used for the planting beds as
well as for the sandbox

A

B

C

D

A plant containers made of the same steel panel

B a staircase mediates between the building and
   the courtyard area

C ground level fountain

D view of the whole Courtyard

A

B

Nicolaas Beetsplein

Design:	DS (Maike van Stiphout, Jana Crepon) & NL architects (Kamiel Klaasse)
Location:	Dordrecht, The Netherlands
Client:	City Council of Dordrecht
Completion:	2006
Size:	10.000 m^2
Costs:	852.000 €
Photographs:	Aeliane van den Ende

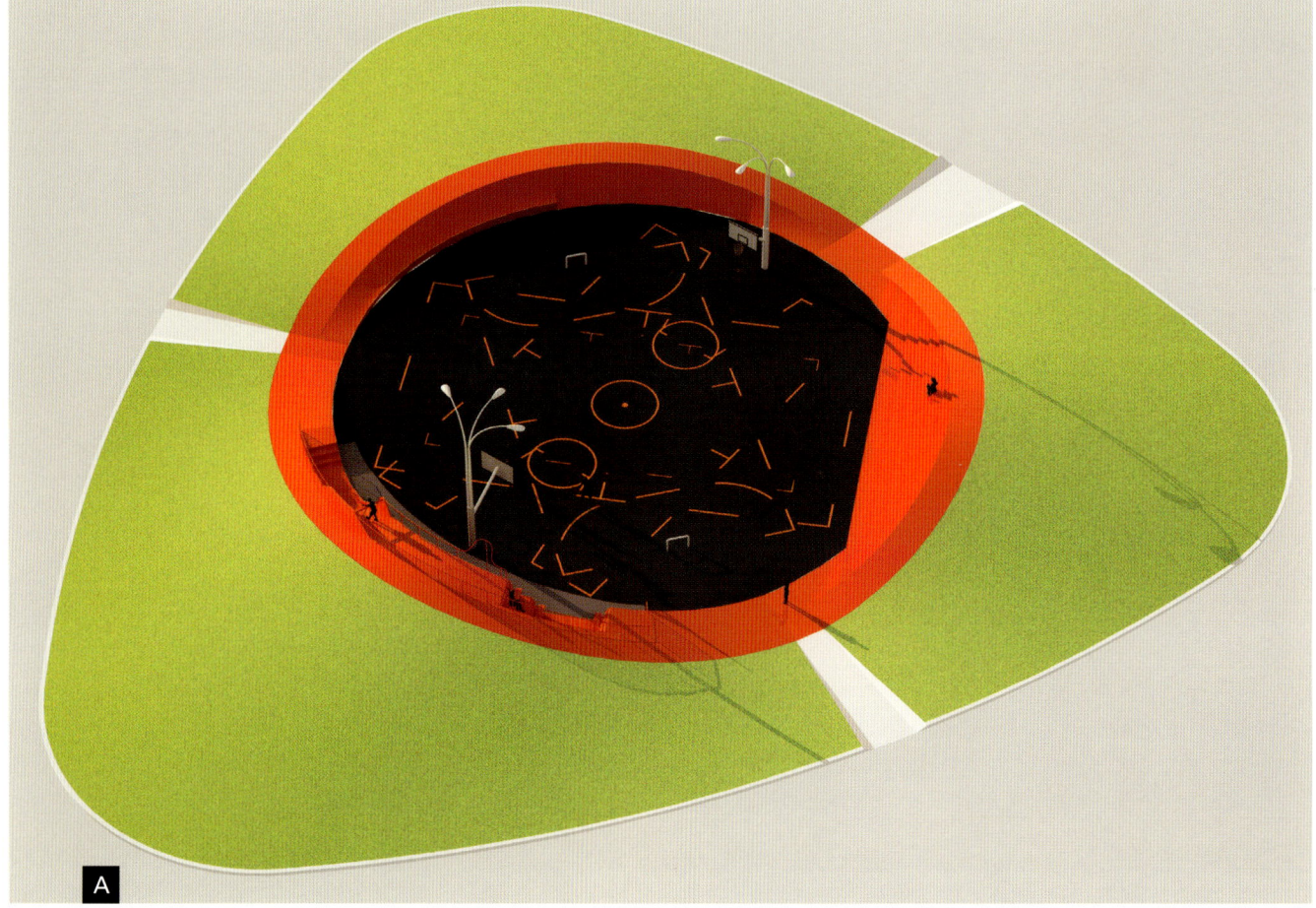

A

Design play ring with green slope Oud Krispijn, a district in the city of Dordrecht, was once set up as a garden village. Because of demolition new space arises for green squares. One of these is Nicolaas Beetsplein.

Small children, adolescents and the elderly inhabitants are the target groups of this new square. For small children a safe and captivating play area is created, for the adolescents it is a place to play sports. For other inhabitants the square makes a peaceful meeting place with sufficient seats. Due to its dimension and central position within the district the new Nicolaas Beetsplein has a coordinating function for the neighborhood, it has become a place for events like concerts, markets, fairs and local festivals. From the center of the square to the fringe the following zones can be distinguished:

1. Sports and play program in the centre, with maximum distance to the facades, but still visible. This zone offers the possibility to play soccer, basketball, to skate and to ice skate in the winter.
2. Various play-, sport- and sit elements are integrated in the fringe of the square. The sloping lawn gives the square a green character.
3. An informal fringe zone, used by different target groups alternating and casually passing.
4. Parking places on the outside of the road, framed by trees and hedges
5. Extra broad pavement and hedges in front of the facades, a pleasant square fringe for the inhabitants.

B

A plan

B a fence that becomes sliding pole

A

B

C

D

A-D the new playing ground gives the neighborhood
children a smart place to relate to, whilst
offering a soft, green view to the elderly people
that live in the surrounding houses

A

B

C

A yard southward
B yard eastward
C yard, view on the mosaic pavement

Residential Building Riem

Landscape:	Landschaftsarchitekt Wendler
Architect:	Sampo Widman
Location:	Munich Riem, Germany
Client:	Gewofag Munich
Completion:	2004
Size:	5.300 m^2
Costs:	600.000 €
Photographs:	Hubert Wendler

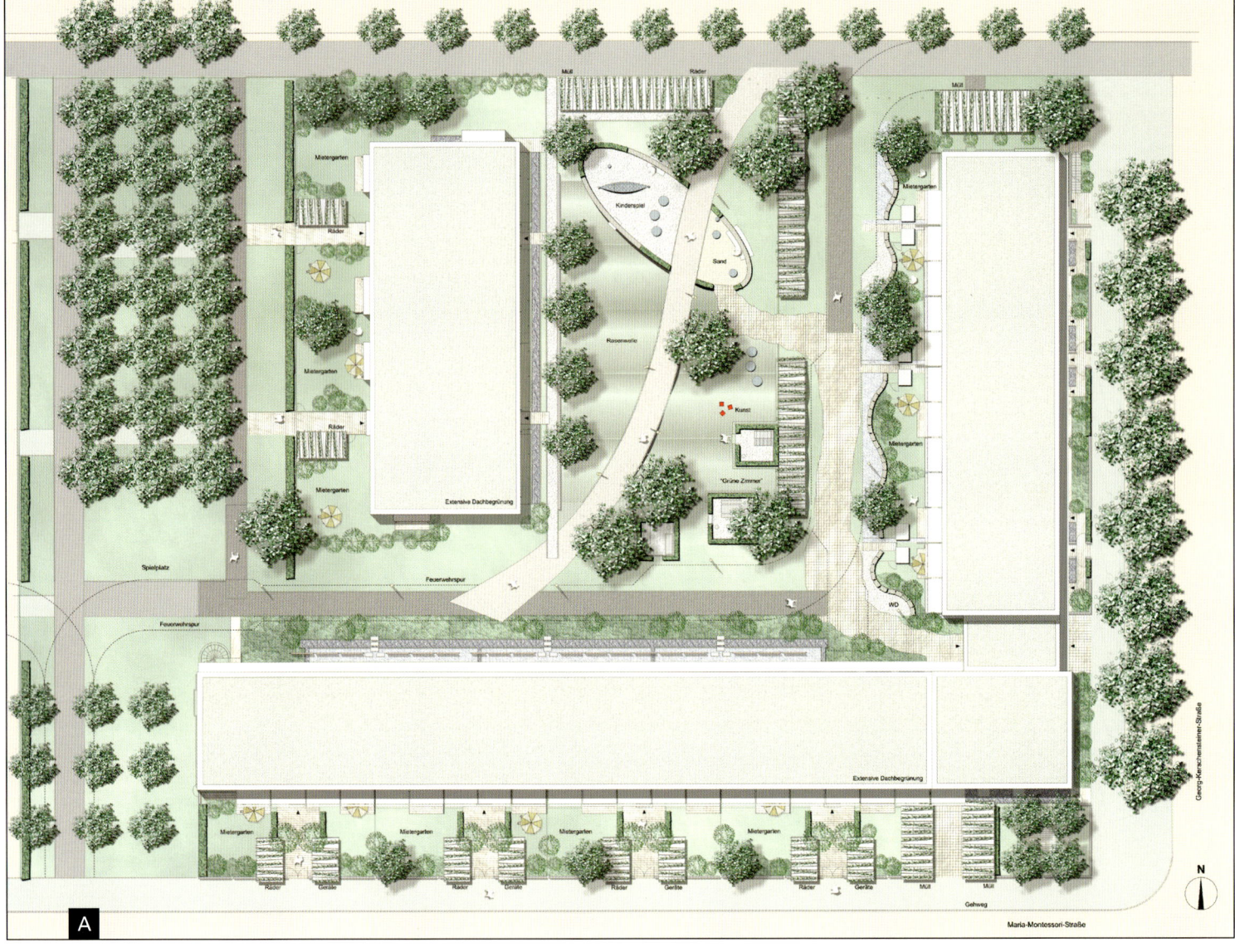

Diagonal cut through green waves"

The design was developed by contrasting waveforms from the strict edges of the surrounding town planning. It was intended to create an easy atmosphere with qualities in the detail.

A yard out of waved lawn and metal roofs between the housing and a parking garage is crossed by a diagonal alley. The lawn-waves prevent brawly and spanning ball games, but advance individual play. Embedded in the yard there is an elliptical playground, which is composed of a sandpit a wall for climbing and hiding.

Squares of hedges with integrated benches and a playhouse for kids facilitate an untroubled stay in the yard. The garden parts for private use are separated by blinds and plants from each other and the public green. Trenches for retaining rainwater build a natural border between private gardens and the yard.

B

C

A site plan

B yard northward

C green waves

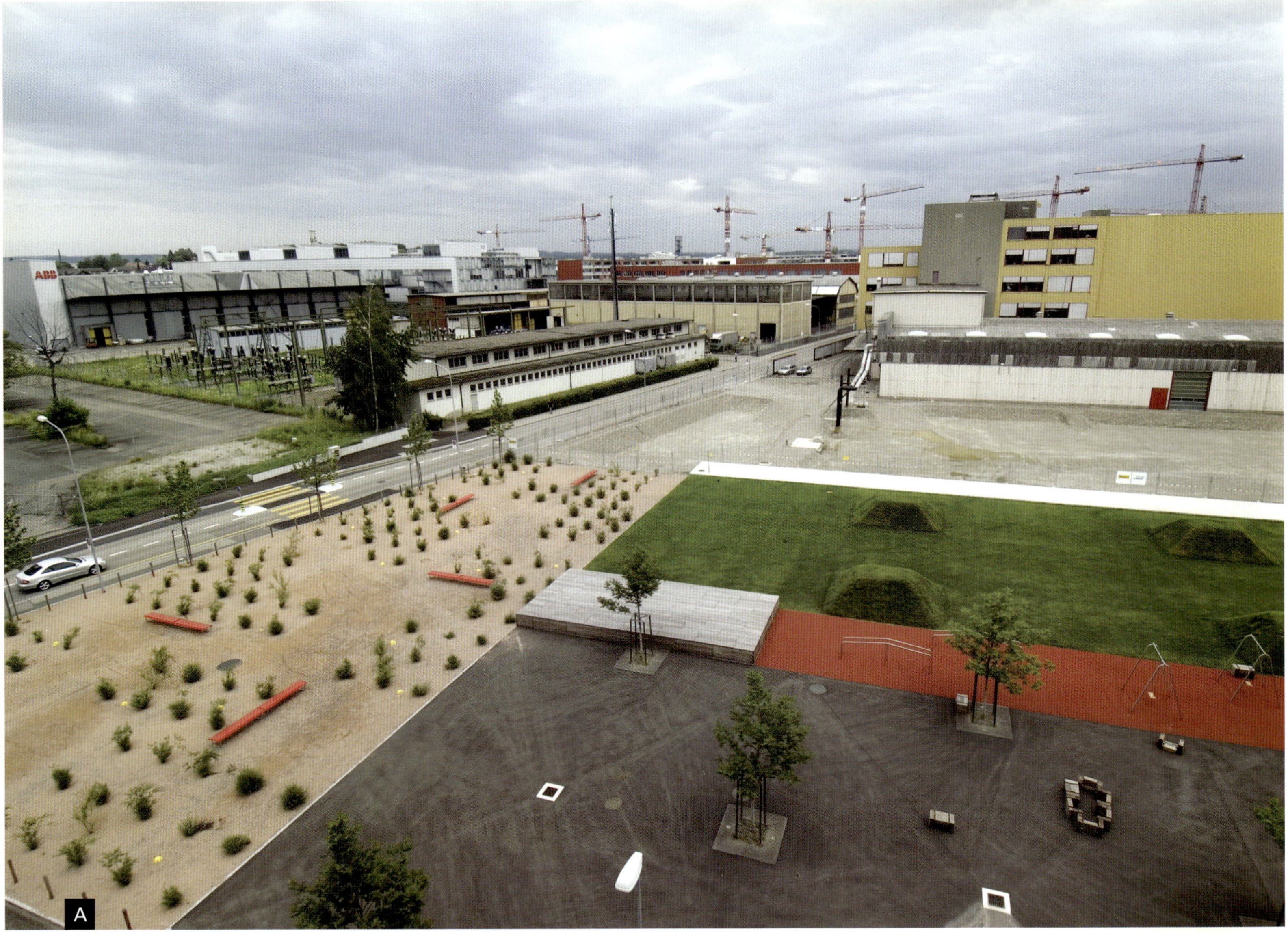

A

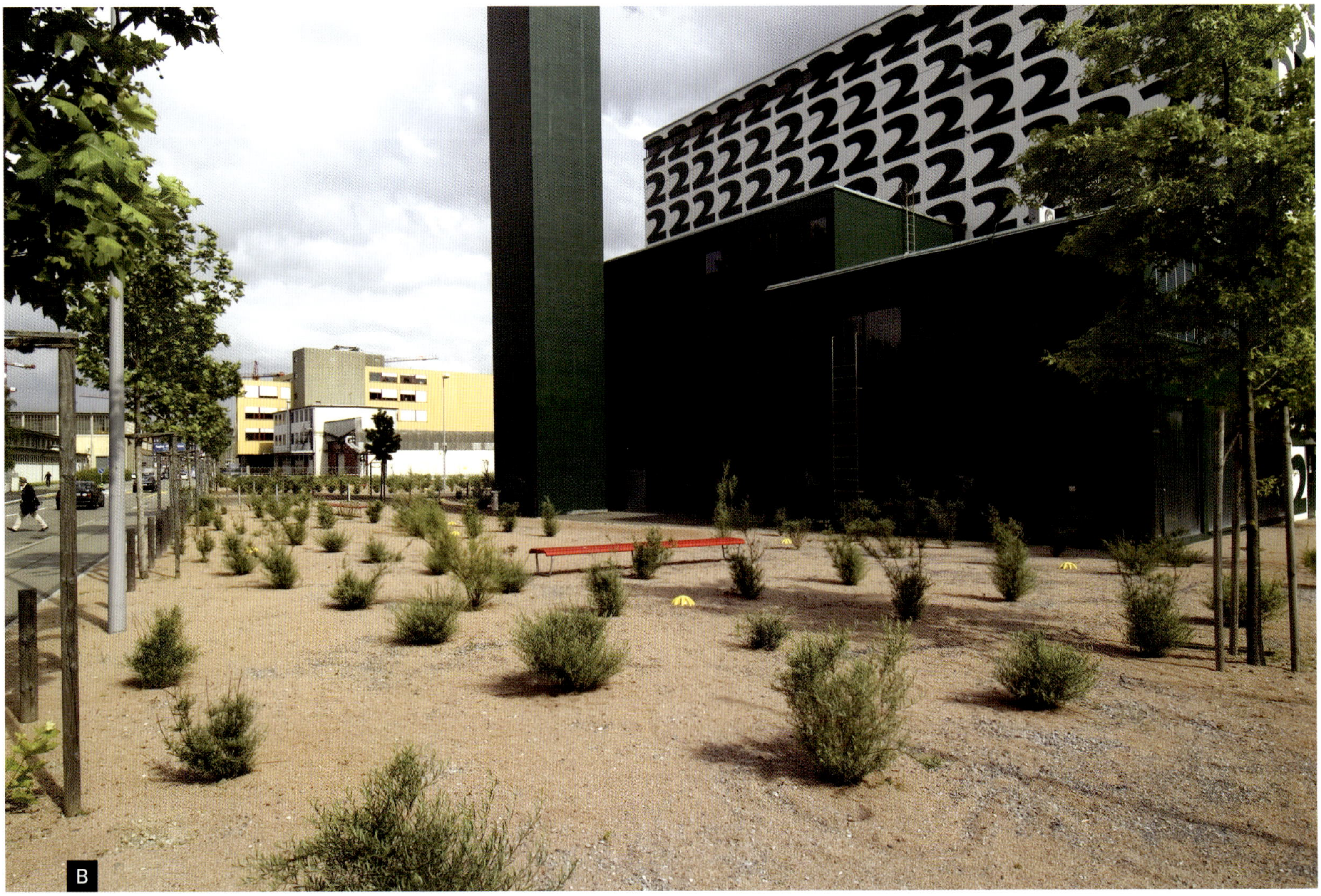

B

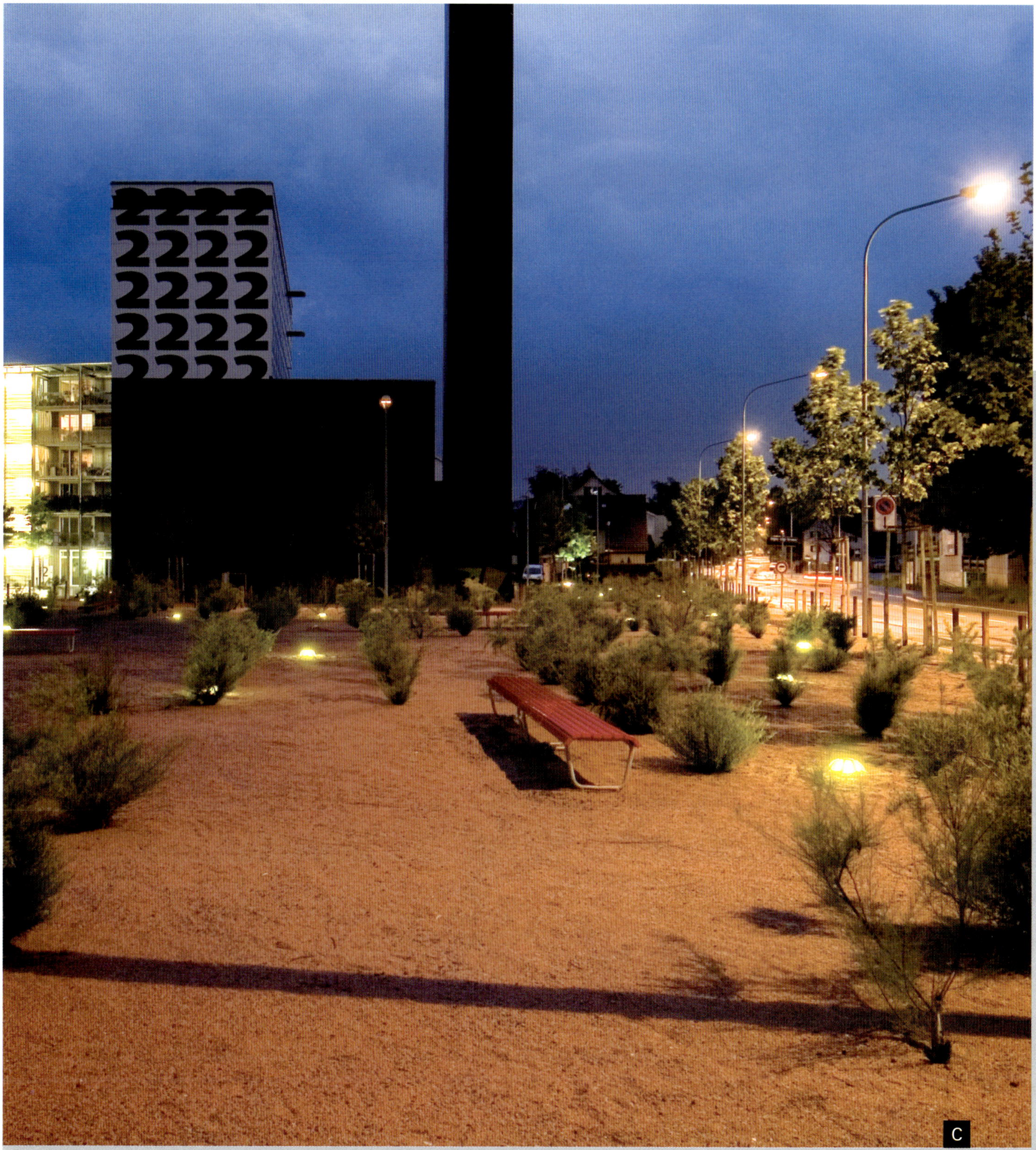

A overview of the park
B gravel field with power station in the background
C illuminate gravel field at night

Louis-Häfliger-Park

Landscape: KuhnTruninger Landschaftsarchitekten
Location: Zurich, Switzerland
Client: Civil Engineering and Recycling Departement Zurich
Completion: 2003
Size: 130.000 m^2
Costs: 2.500.000 CHF
Photographs: KuhnTruninger Landschaftsarchitekten

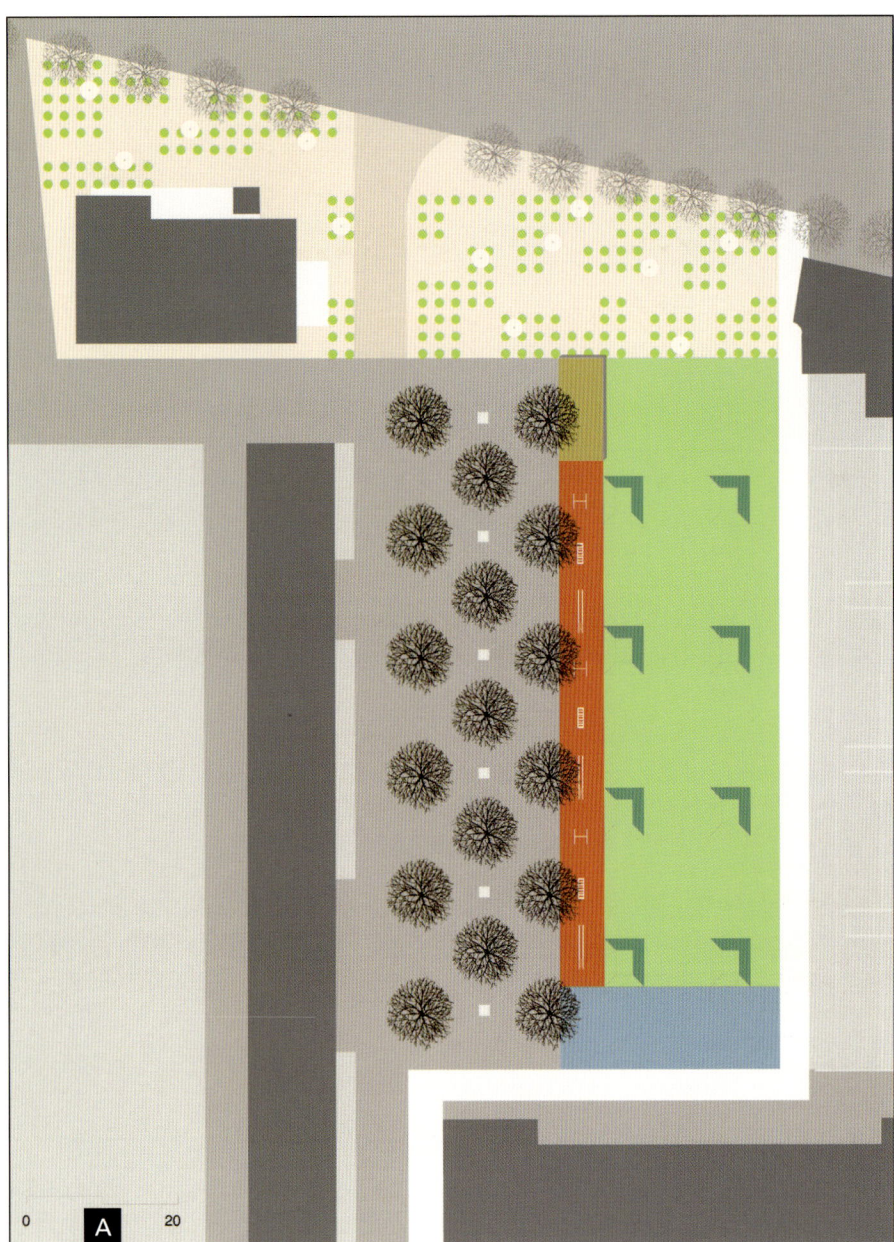

0 A 20

The Louis-Häfliger-park is located between an industry and living area. The design concept is based on the abolition of the boundaries between park, industry and residential area.

The park is composed of fields, which are developing from the heterogeneous borders and refer to the immediate vicinity by its materials, shape and dimension.

An existing power station is integrated into the park by the gravel field. A grid of willow shrubs forms a common area and appears as a filter to the Binzmühle Street. The effect is supported by a ground lamp normally used as street lighting.

The asphalt square is developed out of the roadside environment of the Regina-Kägi-Street. Wing nuts trees (Pterocarya fraxinifolia) which are classic park trees emphasize the hybrid character of this field between square and park. The modeling of the asphalt surface notifies the rain water drain in this area which has a high water level. Heavy rain creates temporary geometric water surfaces.

The stereo metric formed grass sculptures in the lawn field remind of the former existing ammunition depots of the Oerlikon Contraves Company.

A sport cage, the "belt of games" with a rhythmic sequence of game and climbing gear as well as the wood deck useful as stage or common area are additional typical requests of a park. Cubical wood stools can be used both as seats and as game sculptures.

A	master plan
B	the "belt of games" between meadow and a field of trees
C	view of form the top to the blue field

B

C

A

A seat objects are lift out of the wood deck
B a wood deck covert the asphalt to emphasize the common area

Old Print Factory

Landscape:	relais Landschaftsarchitekten
Architect:	zymara und loitzenbauer architektur
Location:	Hannover, Germany
Client:	Klasing Karacay Klasing GbR
Completion:	2005
Size:	450 m^2
Costs:	50.000 €
Photographs:	Stefan Müller

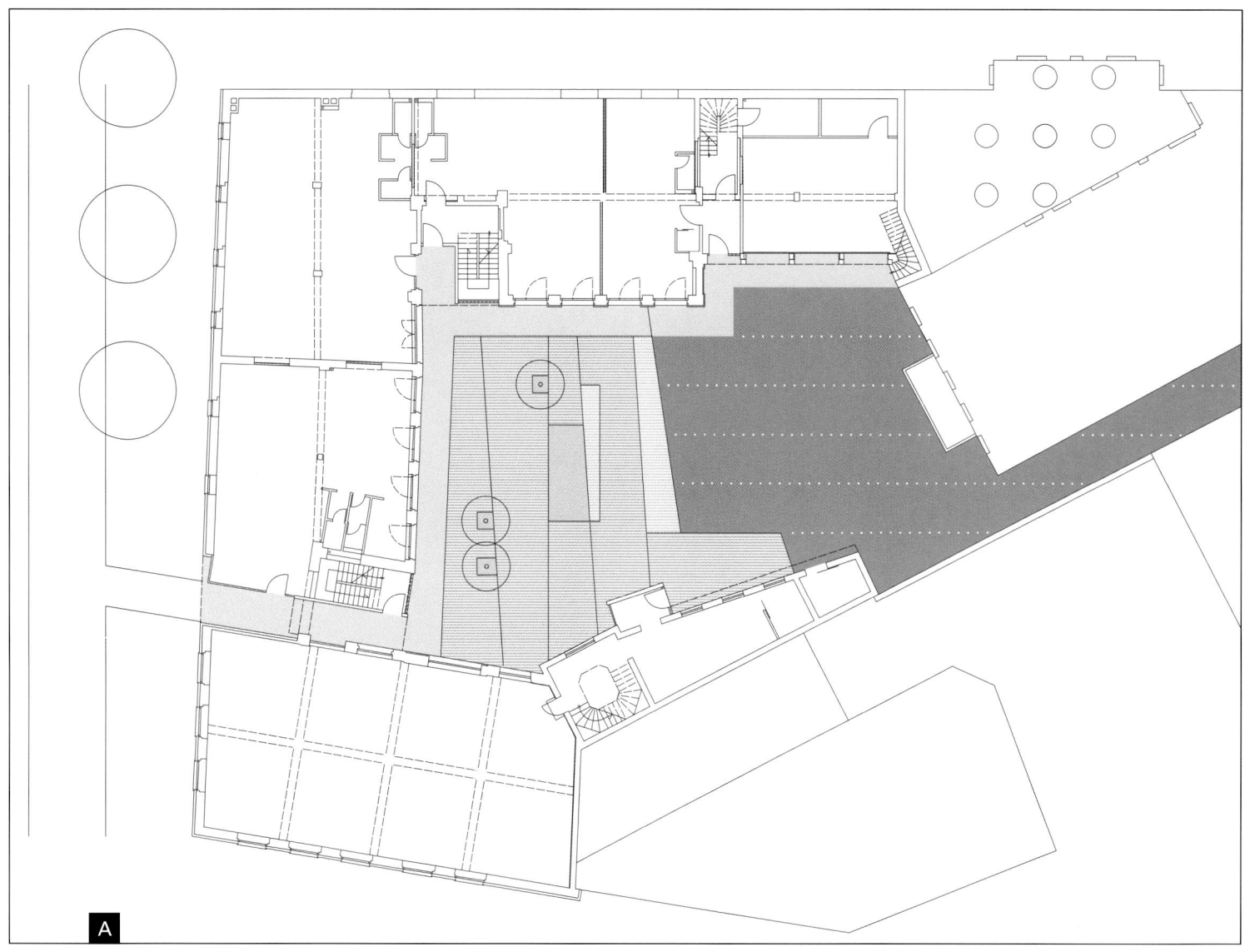

The former area a print factory is rebuilt to a modern work and living place. The 2-3 storey building surrounds a courtyard which is connected though a gateway with the outside area to the street.

A new designed gateway opens the courtyard to the adjacent park and university. The courtyard forms the heart piece of the ensemble. Dwellings, studio and office units of different size are orient with accesses and windows to the yard.

The courtyard area is overstretched by a wood deck and covers the existing asphalt. The wood deck formulated a common area which is slightly lifted up compare to the roadside area. Seat objects are lift out of the horizontal wood lathing, a sinking forms a sandpit area. Ornamental plants in umbrella forms (Amelanchier lamarckii) throw its shadow in loose distribution on the wood deck.

A	master plan
B	a sinking in the wood deck forms the sand pit
C	view over the wood deck

B

C

A overview of the central area of the Park. Multifunctional grassed areas
B secondary path in fine gravel and stone setts

Tejo and Trancão Park

Landscape:	João Ferreira Nunes
Location:	Lisbon / Loures, Portugal
Client:	EXPO'98 Park S.A.
Completion:	1998
Size:	900.000 m^2
Costs:	12.000.000 €
Photographs:	Leonardo Finotti

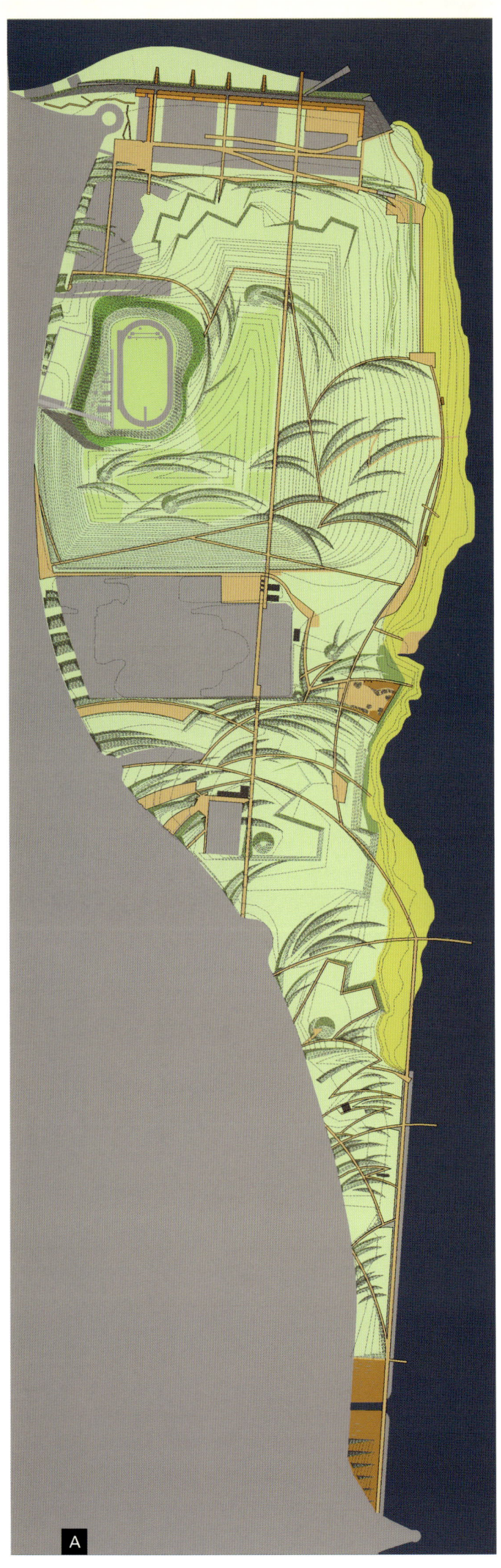

A

The Tejo and Trancão Park covers approximately 90ha of riverside area on the right bank of the river Tejo, from the Vasco da Gama Tower, located on the southern boundary of the park, to the Trancão river, which forms it's northern boundary, encompassing the EXPO'98 intervention area.

A set of profoundly marking activities, regrettably characteristic of town boundary situations, the sanitary landfill site and Beirolas Sewage Treatment Plant (deactivated industrial units), the indiscriminate use of the site as a dumpsite, the unacceptable levels of pollution in the Trancão, the Vasco da Gama Bridge construction site depot, converged in defining an exceptional landscape and environmental disqualification. This set of situations occurs in the immediate vicinity of the Tejo's Estuary Natural Reserve, a site of unwavering ecological e landscape potential.

The obstacles to the establishment of a green urban park were not constrained to the previously mentioned hindrances; the geotechnical situation predicted the occurrence of differentiated soil compactions, particularly in a substantial strip along the riverside and in the northern area, near the Trancão.

The proposal aimed to establish a spatial organisation that offered great scenic, visual and sensorial diversity, sustained by a structure which reflects the coherence and formal unity in the perception of the broad intervention.

The formalisation of the structure results in the combination of three distinctly hierarchic elements:

- The landforms represent the fundamental landscape structuring element, shaping ecological, scenic and use consequences, which establish the meaning of the prospective landscape: three-dimensional, diversified, rhythmic. These landforms, particularly the wind formed ones, define, due to their relative layout and orientation, not merely a formal score, but, above all, an ecological rhythm that is repeated throughout the park, essentially by means of the contrast between gentle facing slopes and the abrupt north facing ones.

- Planting zones and plant cover accentuate this contrast, coinciding typologies and specific floristic sets with matching ecological situations, anticipating, image wise, the result that time and nature would eventually take upon themselves to establish. Given that what is intended is an intensely lived park, the introduced systems are necessarily artificial in order to withstand a suitable ecological load.

- The path system composes a hierarchical network that defines, in itself, an autonomous structure, functional, subsidiary to the three dimensional structure with which it is articulated in an indissoluble manner.

B

C

A master plan

B wooden path/bridge that connects the Expo 98
area and the Park

C wooden path in the wetland area

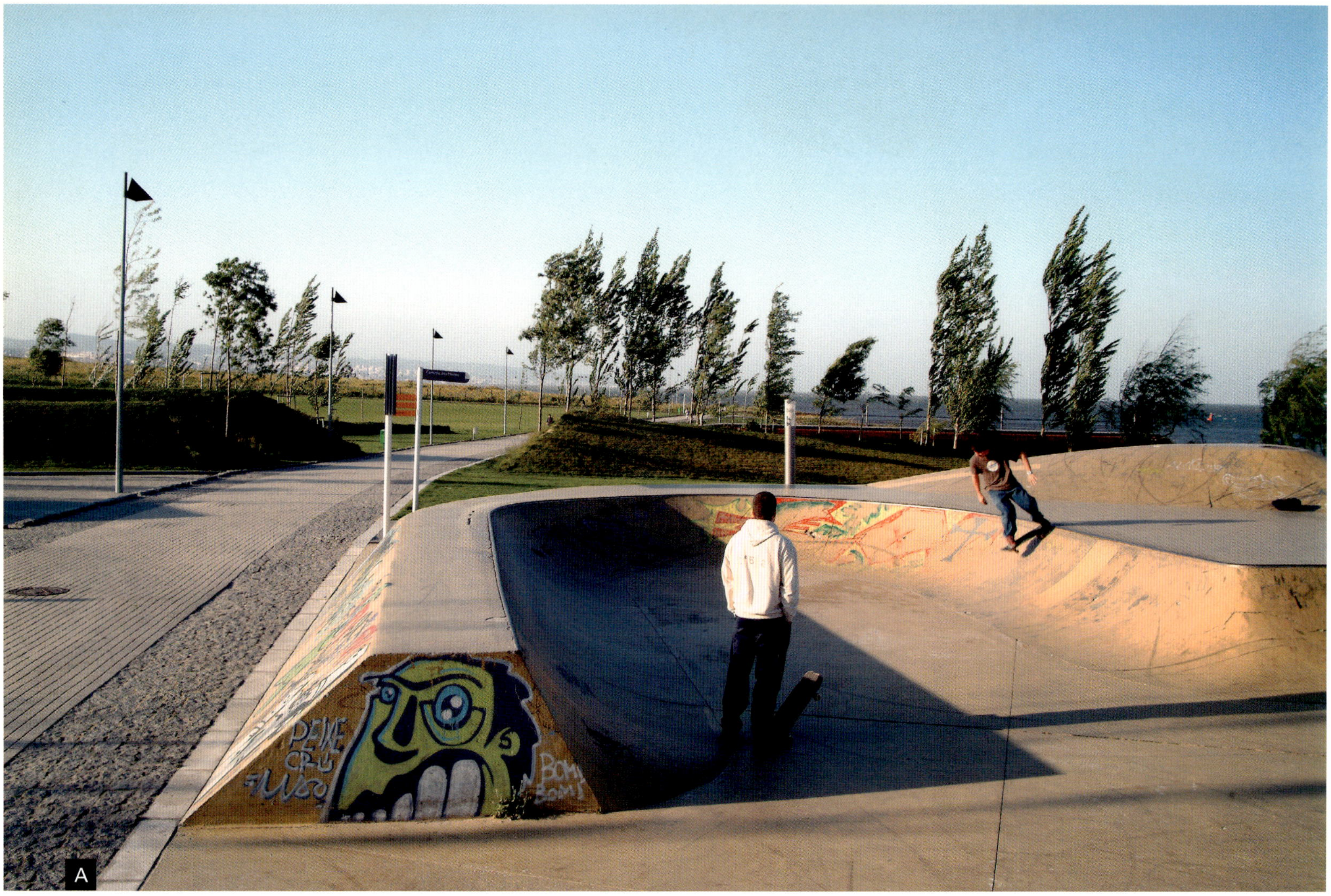
A

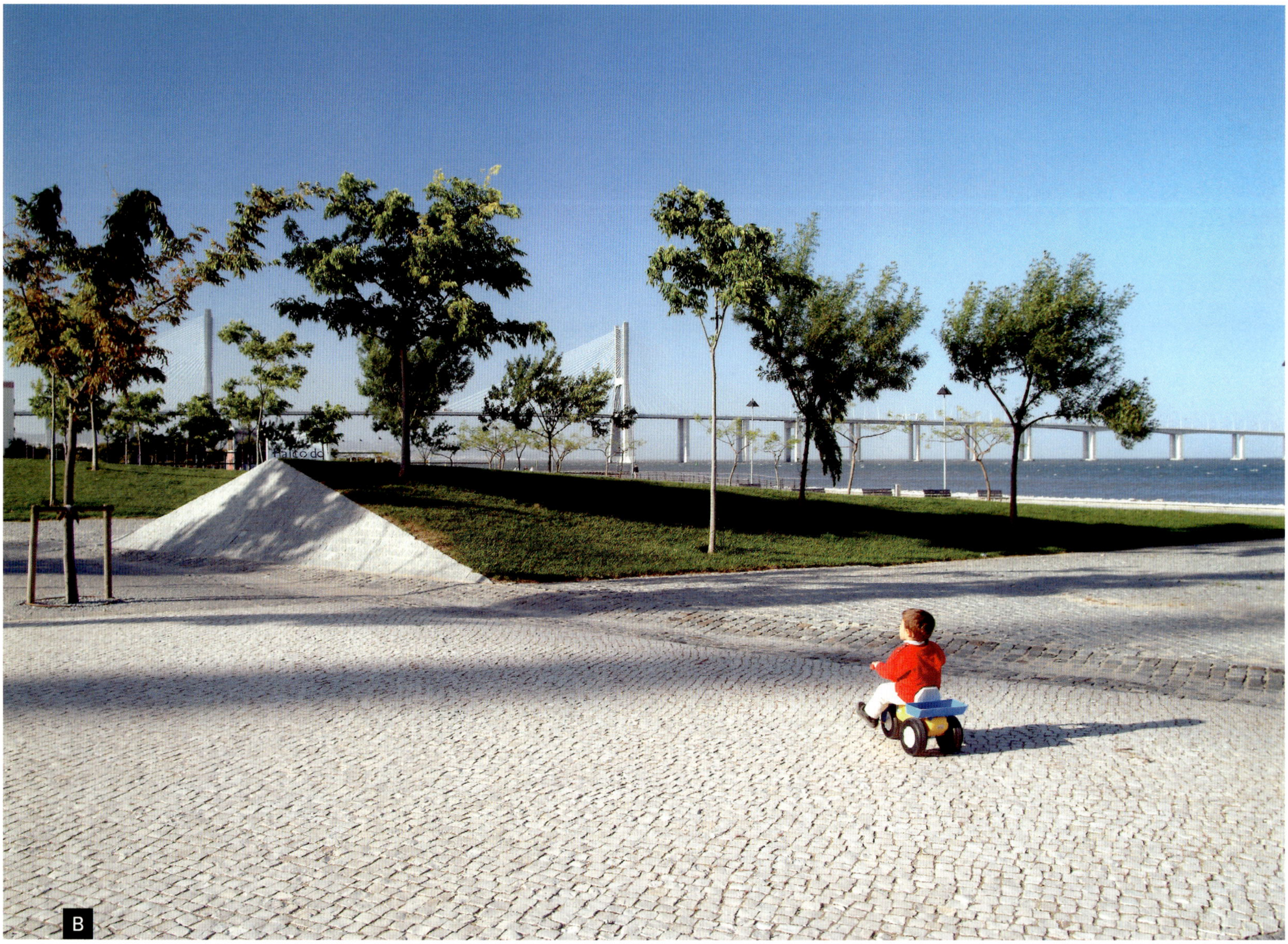
B

A concrete Skate Park

B Tejo and Trancão Park south plaza

C main path of the Tejo and Trancão Park

A

B

A new building of the Hans-Otto-Theater
B the Hans-Otto-Theater right on the waterfront of the
   Tiefes Lake

Schiffbauergasse (Ship Builder Lane) Potsdam

Architect:	Johannes Grothaus
Location:	Potsdam, Germany
Client:	City of Potsdam
Completion:	2004
Size:	2.0 ha
Costs:	2.500.000 €
Photographs:	Johannes Grothaus

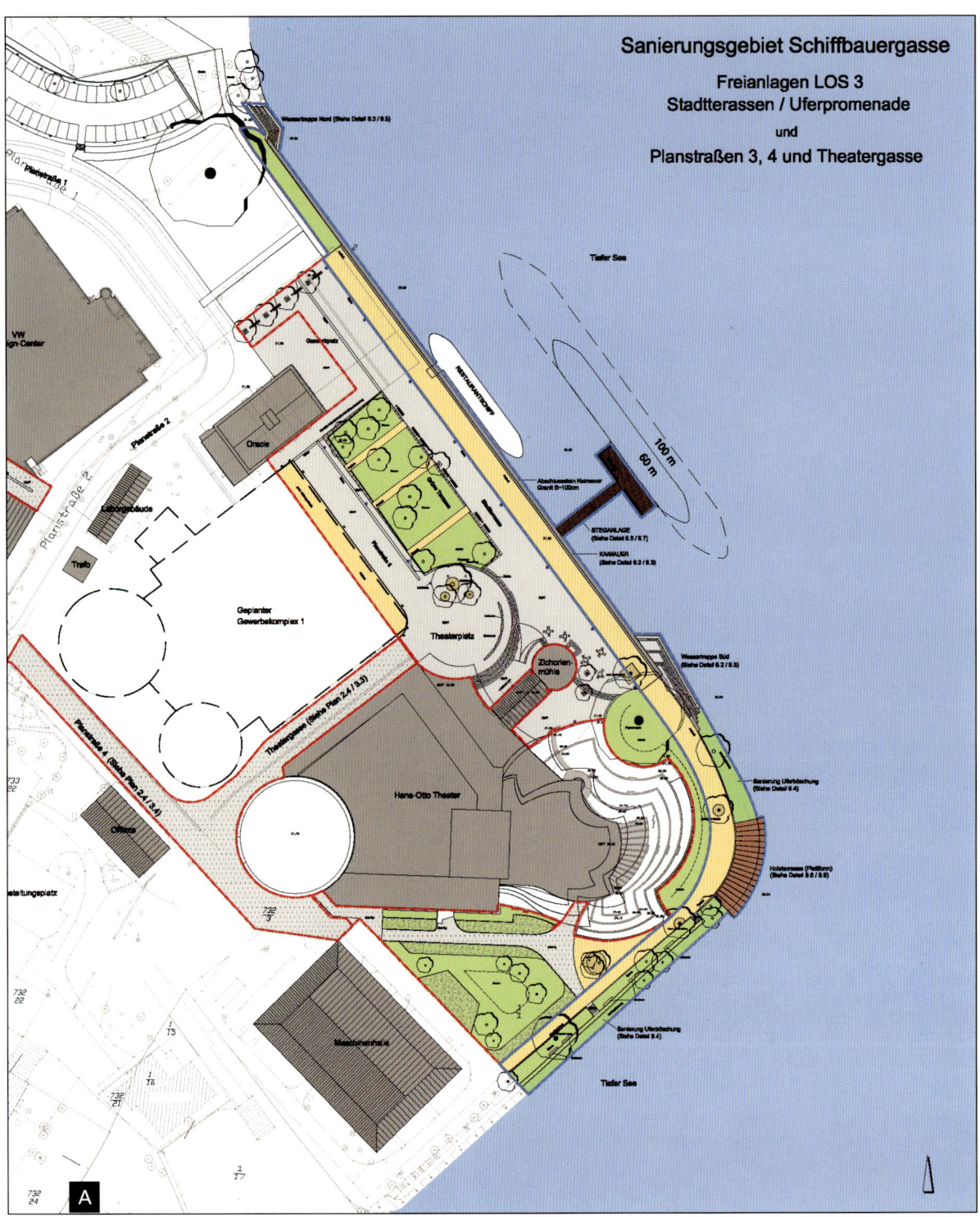

The culture site Schiffbauergasse is situated on the shore of the Tiefer See and will be developed in one of the most exposed locations of Potsdam's cultural landscape. The main projects are the construction of the Hans-Otto-Theater and of several commercial buildings, including the Volkswagen Design Center. Main aspects of the open space planning are the "Stadtterrasse" stretching from the main entrance of the theater to the lakeside and the waterfront promenade.

B

C

A master plan

B lawn terraces with view to the Volkspark
Babelsberg

C seat steps as transition to the lawn terrace
reach the water

A

B

C

D

A city terrace with birch trees and waterfront promanade

B ship landing-stage as "place on the water" with a bench

C lawn terraces with view to a suburb of Potsdam

D wood deck offer a view to the urban and landscape scenery

B

A the Access to the boat level formed by ramp and staircases
B panoramic view to the historic centre of Spandau

Spandau Havel Promenade

Landscape:	HÄFNER/JIMENEZ
Project Team:	Thomas Jarosch, Alexander Heinrich
Location:	Berlin, Germany
Client:	Water City Berlin GmbH
Completion:	2001
Size:	11.000 m²
Costs:	2.320.000 €
Photographs:	Thomas Jarosch, Winfried Häfner, Wasserstadt GmbH

Public open spaces in the residential area of Haveleck, defined in the statutory development plans as pedestrian zones, were the object of a competition carried out by the Wasserstadt Spandau housing development agency in 1999. Five landscape architecture practices were invited to examine an exposed public open space with multiple connections and views across the banks of the Havel River. The goal of the competition was to present a design concept at an implementation level that met current functional and economic demands and convincingly answered future urban development, architecture and landscape planning needs.

In general, our firm opted for a simple and precise design such as is usually characteristic of our projects that are near a large surface of water, since the water and the visual relationships with it strongly affect the development.

With this project, the historical uses of the site presented some unique problems. First, the area had served as a port for more than 200 years. Subsequently, during the 40 years that Berlin was a divided city, the area held fuel installations to guarantee fuel supply during blockades. This resulted in severe contamination of the subsoil by cyanide. After the wall fell, since the area was no longer needed for storage purposes, the Wasserstadt plan was introduced. Located on the edge of the Havel River and facing west with excellent views of the setting sun, this area seemed an ideal recreational space.

Because of the cyanide in the subsoil, it was necessary to design the promenade in two levels, one at the height of the sheet pile wall and another at the level of future urban development, some three metres higher. The difference in height between the two levels had to be resolved in a way that was both functional and also connected the levels to guarantee access. This demand was met by a 30 metre wide staircase that opens the plaza onto the river and the jetty. In this design, we found inspiration in the usual details of river constructions in Berlin. Thus, the boxes of staircases at the end of the small streets in the urban development reflect those found along the city's river routes.

With its rigid symmetry, the central plaza creates an element that is capable of merging the two parts of the promenade with their different structures. We also installed a prefabricated concrete wall painted orange, highlighting the colour of the old sheet pile wall.

The proposal is impressive in its clear urban zoning of the riverbank into a lower promenade oriented towards the waterfront and a balcony allowing generous prospects across the Havel River. Above, the project boasts a great variety of different recreational spaces of a highly sensual nature such as an exterior staircase with a landing stage, an open plaza, blocks of lime trees and a balcony. The spatial articulation of the promenade is supported by the coherent and harmonious selection of materials.

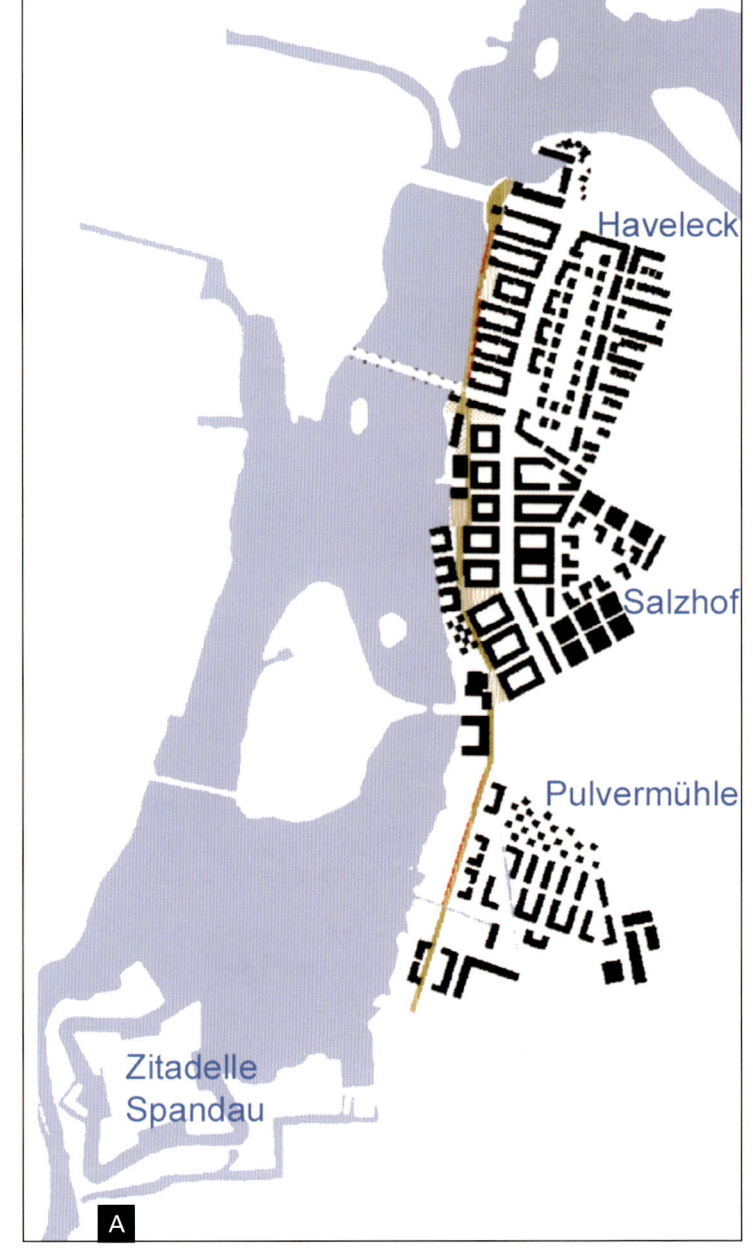

B

C

A master plan

B view of the finished Haveleck residential quarter

C view of the site before building the promenade

A

B

A the lower level at the standing stage

B a large staircase leads to a landing stage at the town plaza

C view to the opposite site of Spandau Lake

D lower part of the promenade

A

B

C

A-B hundreds of people can enjoy the element water
C   spacious squares emphasize the urban character of
     this park at the river

Limmatstufen im Wipkingerpark

Landscape:	asp Landschaftsarchitekten AG
Location:	Zurich, Switzerland
Client:	Civil engineering office Zurich
Completion:	2004
Size:	20.000 m^2
Costs:	4.500.000 SFr
Photographs:	asp Landschaftsarchitekten AG

A

A 180 long composition of steps joining the river Limmat have been set up replacing a high wall along the shore. Through the new design visitors to the park can experience directly the flowing clear water. The concise layout of the construction is matching the rapid urban development of the area.

A site plan - Hand drawing

B the new river design offer space for development and play for an aquatic life

C natural stones with niches offer special space for people as well as plants and animals

B

C

A wooden deck of the Lloydplace marking the entrance
to the harboursite from the city, with the specifically
developed 'flow bench'
B wooden footbridge crossing the former Lloyddock

Old / New Harbour Bremerhaven

Landscape:	LATZ + PARTNER
Location:	Bremerhaven, Germany
Client:	Bean Development Company
Completion:	2008
Size:	100.000 m^2
Costs:	22.000.000 €
Photographs:	Christa Panick, Markus Tollhopf

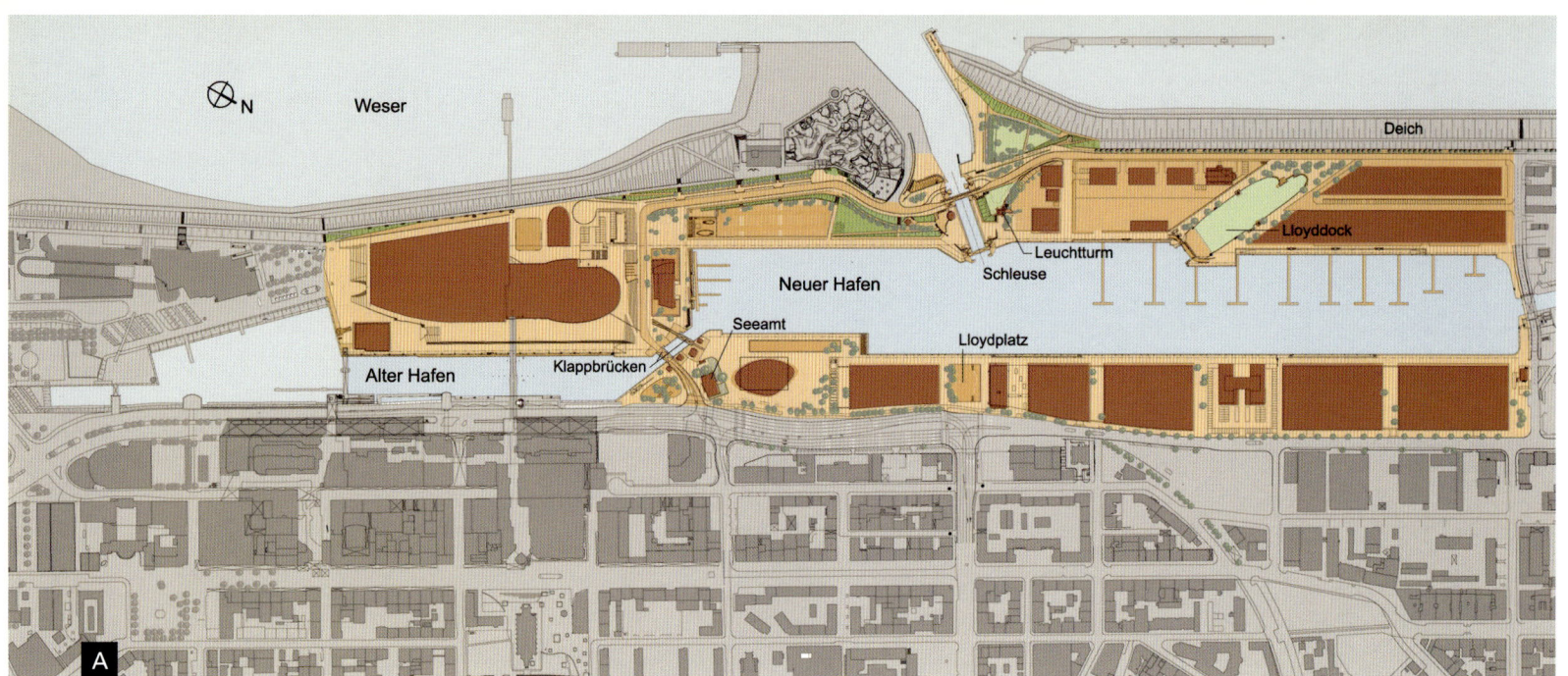

The spatial, ecological and technical renewal of the harbour site becomes the core of a new town quarter. The project follows the strategy of a metamorphosis out of traditional elements. It refers to the existing urban pattern to guarantee a long-term use and development. It works with existing climatic conditions as a positive identity. It aims at establishing a strong language of forms for manifold demands. It works with surface materials common in the place, thus characterizing it with a continuous carpet of natural stone and taking into consideration modern, functional and esthetic tasks. Like inlays or step-stones particular materials are marking special spots.

The quays are zoned by use of material and equipment. Sawn paving stones with smooth surfaces cover the main walking areas whereas the rough surfaces of cobbled zones along the edges of the quays signal "attention" and caution for pedestrian traffic. Also here street furniture and drainage elements were developed especially for this space and emphasize the specific character of the quays. New multifunctional poles have replaced the old streetlamps.

The Lloyd Place is one of the first inlays or step-stones with in the stone carpet and represents the entrance to the harbour. Situated within the Lloyd Street axis it forms the center of an important sightline from the city to the river and the historic lighthouse. With its wooden materials the place offers a warm and inviting atmosphere in the rough maritime climate.

The deck of the Lloyd Place rised nearly 20 cm above the stone carpet. Oaks, hornbeams and wingnuts grow out of the wooden surface. Like all the other equipment of the site, a special bench with modular design has been developed for the place: The Flow Bench is both, seat and sculpture.

During festivities a lattice pylon 16m high illuminates the deck with a flat-top radiator and decorative lighting.

B

C

A master plan Old/New Harbour Bremerhaven

B night view of the harbour

C view from the Loschen Tower upon the
   renewed quays

A

A courtyard with rainwaterbasin and a „Isle of Contemplation"
B forum of the University of Applied Sciences

University of Applied Sciences

Landscape:	Landschaft Drei, Michael F. Heintze
Architect:	Jockers Architects, Stuttgart
Location:	Osnabrück, Germany
Client:	Federal State Of Niedersachsen
Completion:	2004
Size:	2.5 ha
Costs:	1,200.000 €
Photographs:	Michael F. Heintze

The dialogue with the distinguishing marks of the room is searched consciously. The former parade-ground of the barracks becomes the new campus of The University Of Applied Sciences Osnabrück.

The architecture becomes part of the free space. Building and free space imply each other.

The hyprid typus of archtitecture and free space is not only intended as platform for the new building of the University of Applied Sciences, but also as offensive vantage point for the current assessment of the idea of free space.

A

B

A modell of the new Campus

B courtyard with banches of grass and fountain

A

B

C

A waterbasin as reflector

B island of Contemplation

C demarcation, from traffic / campus

221

A

B

C

A view towards the main entrance of the school building
B courtyard structure is organize by wooden longitudinal
  axises with water elements
C view towards over the courtyard

MPSO Buttikon

Landscape:	Koepfli Partner, Landschaftsarchitekten BSLA
Architect:	Graber und Steiger Architekten ETH BSA SIA
Location:	Buttikon, Switzerland
Client:	School Community Obermarch
Completion:	2002
Size:	22.000 m^2
Costs:	1.500.000 SFr, 945.000 €
Photographs:	H. Helfenstein, S. Koepfli, N. Graber

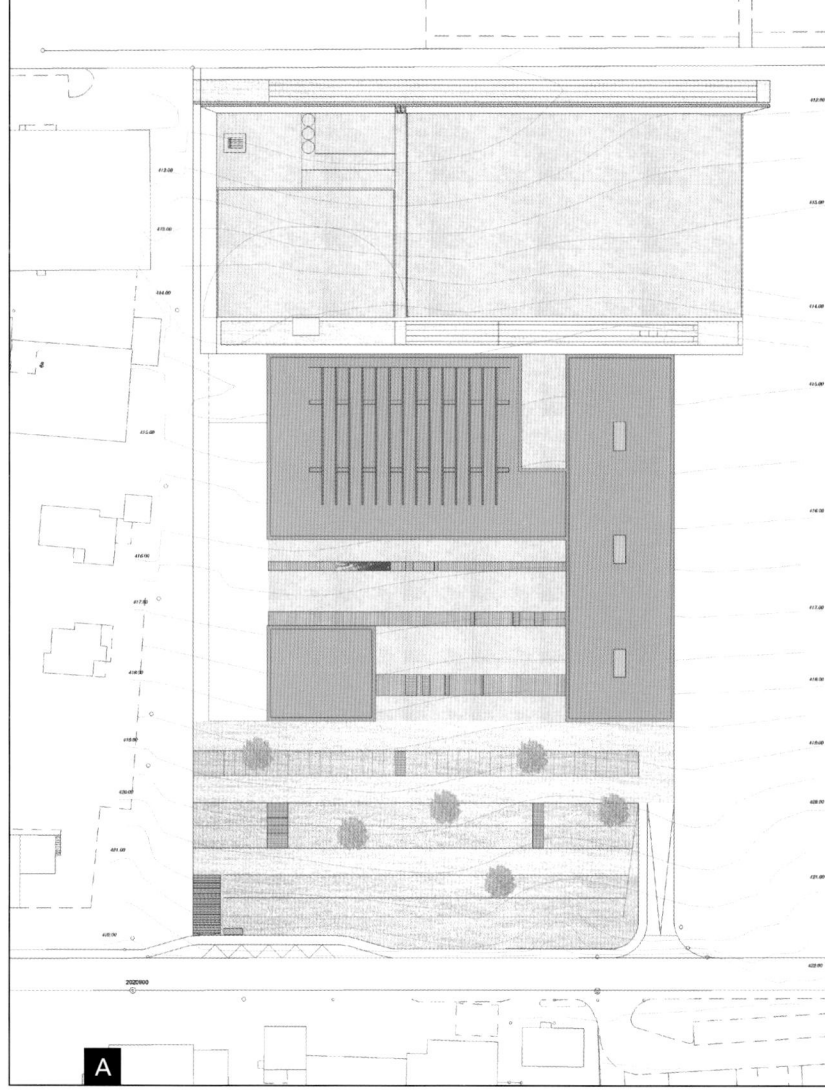

A

The building complex of this district school is set at the rim of the Lint-plain, a former marsh area, whose appearance is characterized by strong linear elements like drainage ditches, embankments and tree hedges as windbreaker.

The aim of the design of this school's environment is to be as much part of the specific landscape as of the buildings architecture.

Just behind the buildings, the terrain rises to the steep slopes of the Glarner Alps, thus the surroundings are already split into two levels. On the upper level, a car park is set in front of the buildings. The sowed in gravel of the parking fields and the macadam of the driveways anticipate the linear rhythm of the main design concept. Willow trees (Salix alba), an exemplary tree of the marshes, provide some shadow.

The concept becomes stricter on the adjacent school yard, which is organized by strips of wooden walkways with platforms. These strips are inspired by the traditional walks of the marshes. The platforms can be used as benches or playing facilities. A shallow pool with reed plants (Typha angustifolia) gives a further reminiscence of the former marshlands.

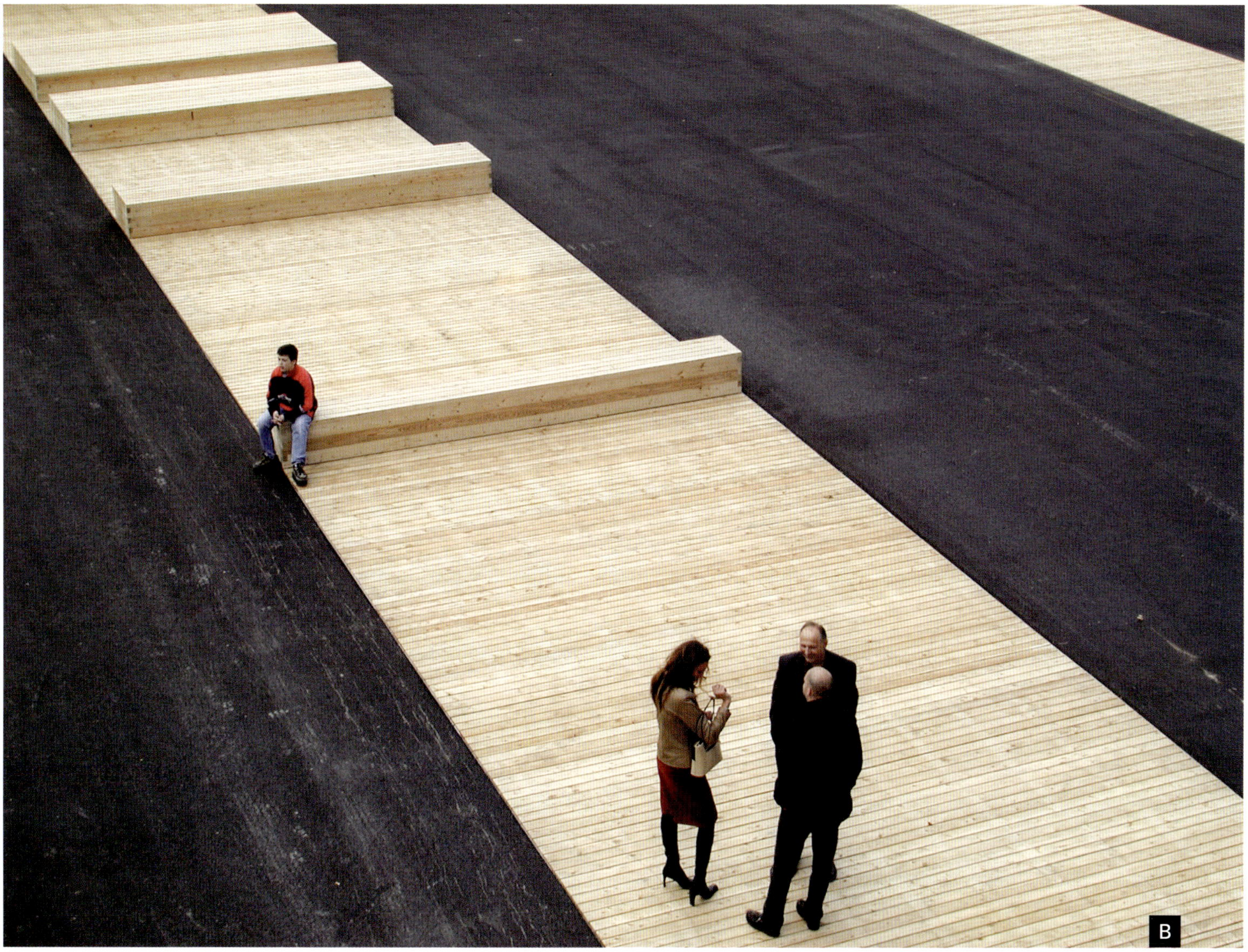

B

C

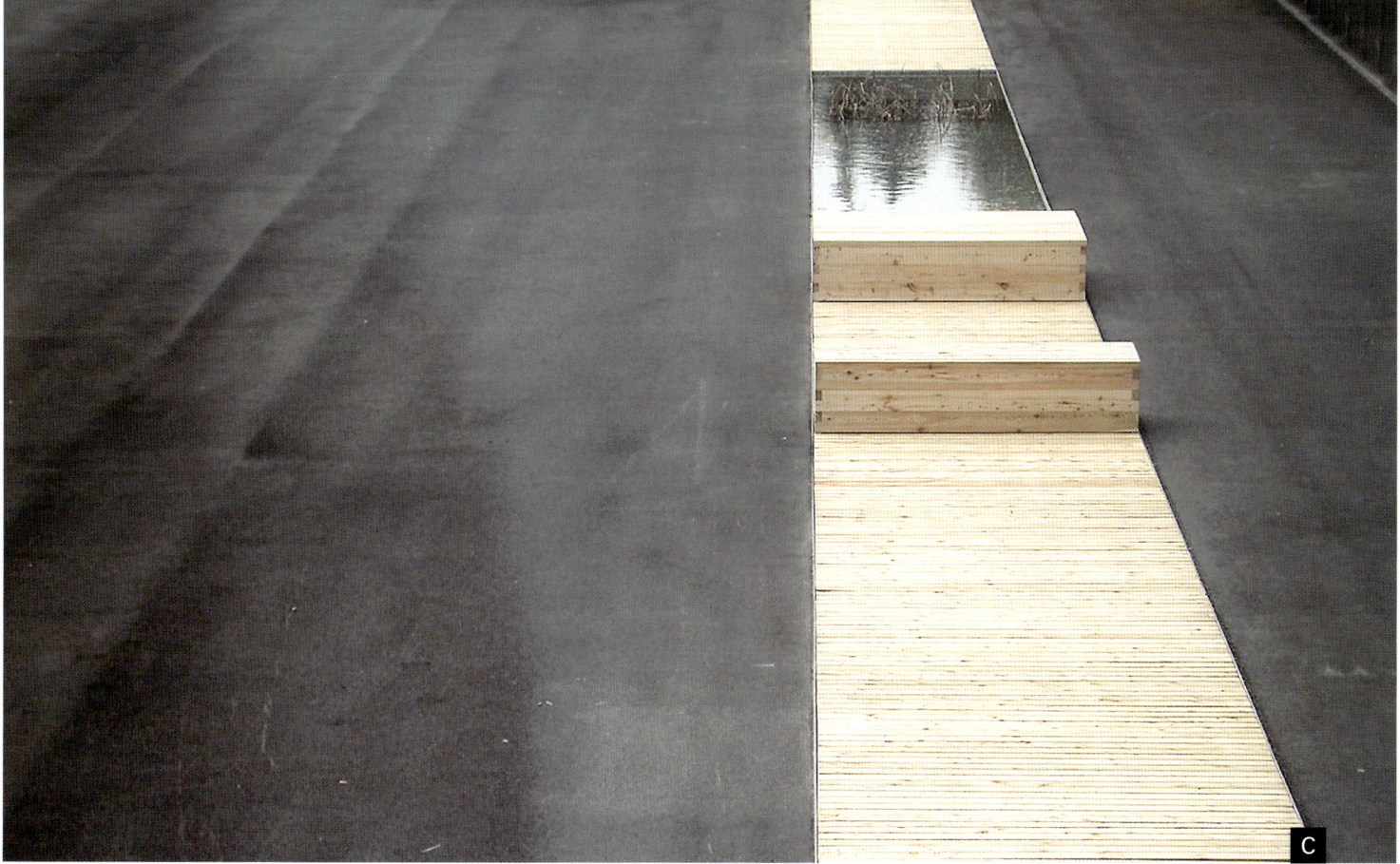

A site plan

B from one of the classrooms on the first floor

C pool with reed plants

A

B

C

A view towards the main entrance of the school building

B passage between the school building and the gym hall

C the transparency of the main entrance links the wooden structure with the surrounding landscape

A

B

C

A-B schoolyard
C   traffic education area

Primaries School at the promenade of freedom

Landscape:	Landschaftsarchitekt Wendler
Architect:	Prof. Krug + Partner
Location:	Munich, Germany
Client:	Bavaria state capital Munich
Completion:	2004
Size:	13.800 m^2
Costs:	755.000 €
Photographs:	Hubert Wendler

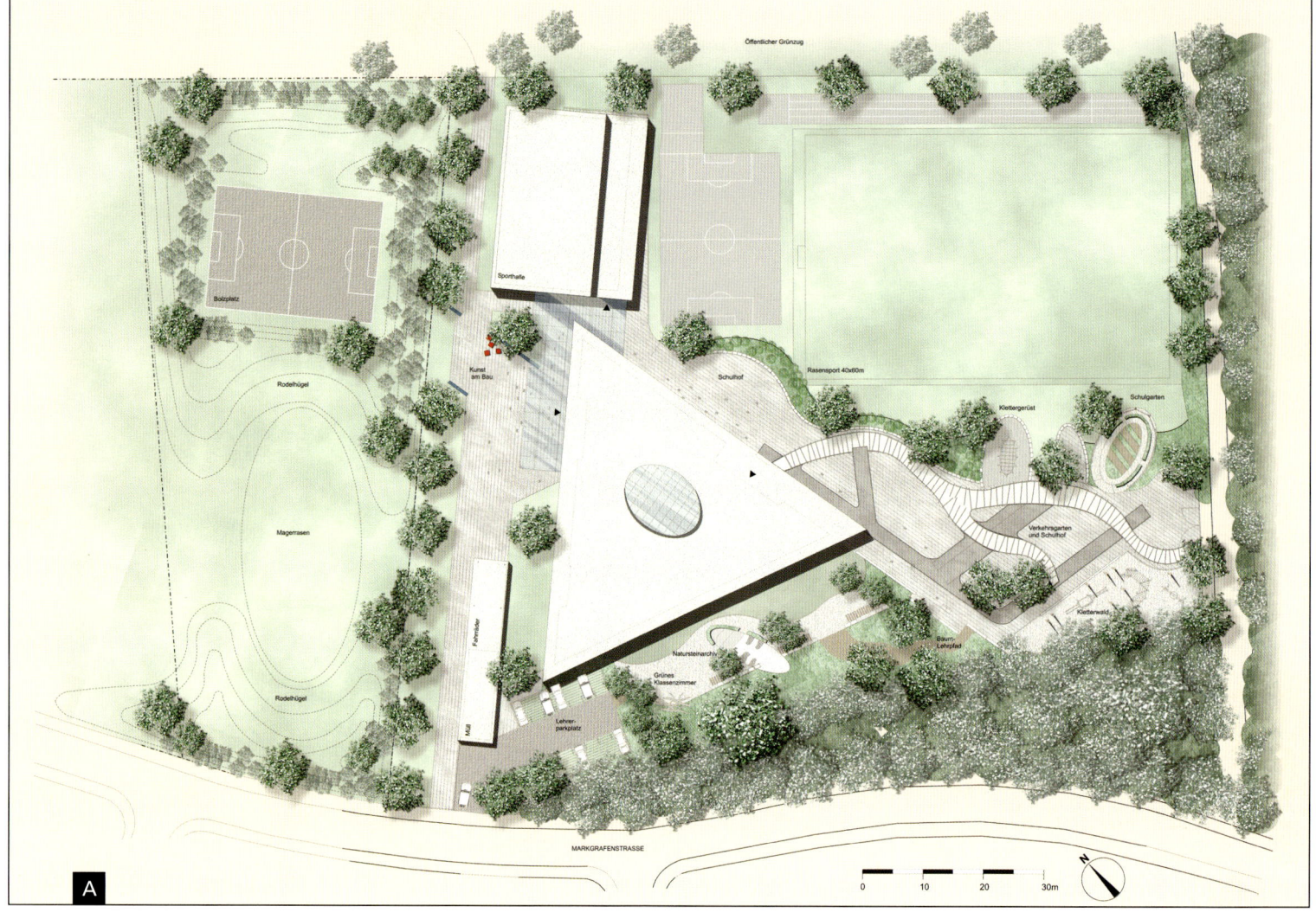

Red dice-chairs and colourful glass elements designed by the artist Bodo Buhl mark the entrance area of the school.

Playful elements which appear to be randomly thrown in have been added to the strict geometric triangular design of the school building. By this small play areas are formed for the children. The required traffic education and exercise zone has been integrated in the large schoolyard in such a way that it can fulfil its function, but does not look like a boring piece of road. Asphalt serves as recognition of a road, but obtains a playful character by its colour as well as coloured crosswalks and arrows.

A school garden and play niches for quiet play and climbing are situated in a waved seating wall made of limestone a red mosaic stones. The wall also separates the playground from the adjacent sports fields.

In the east, a playground made from bare robin trunks sculpturally forms an adventure jungle which is the logical continuation of the adjacent woods. In the south a path for learning about trees and a stone formation as a natural stone archive have been created. The types of natural stones are characteristically for construction in Bavaria and have been labelled accordingly. In the West excavate originated by the school building was modelled as a sledging hill which is also a gathering area for the youth in the recently developed residential area.

B

A site plan

B climbing net

A

B

A playground

B seating wall with mosaic

C natural stone archieve

D schoolgarden

A garden yard „bloom and leaf structure"
B north yard – concrete sculptures
B forecourt main entrance

TU Munich-Garching

Landscape:	Lex-Kerfers Landschaftsarchitekten
Architect:	BMB + P, Munich
Location:	Munich, Germany
Client:	Civil Engineering Department TU Munich
Completion:	2002
Size:	6,6 ha
Costs:	4.500.000 €
Photographs:	Christoph Rehbach, Lex-Kerfers LA

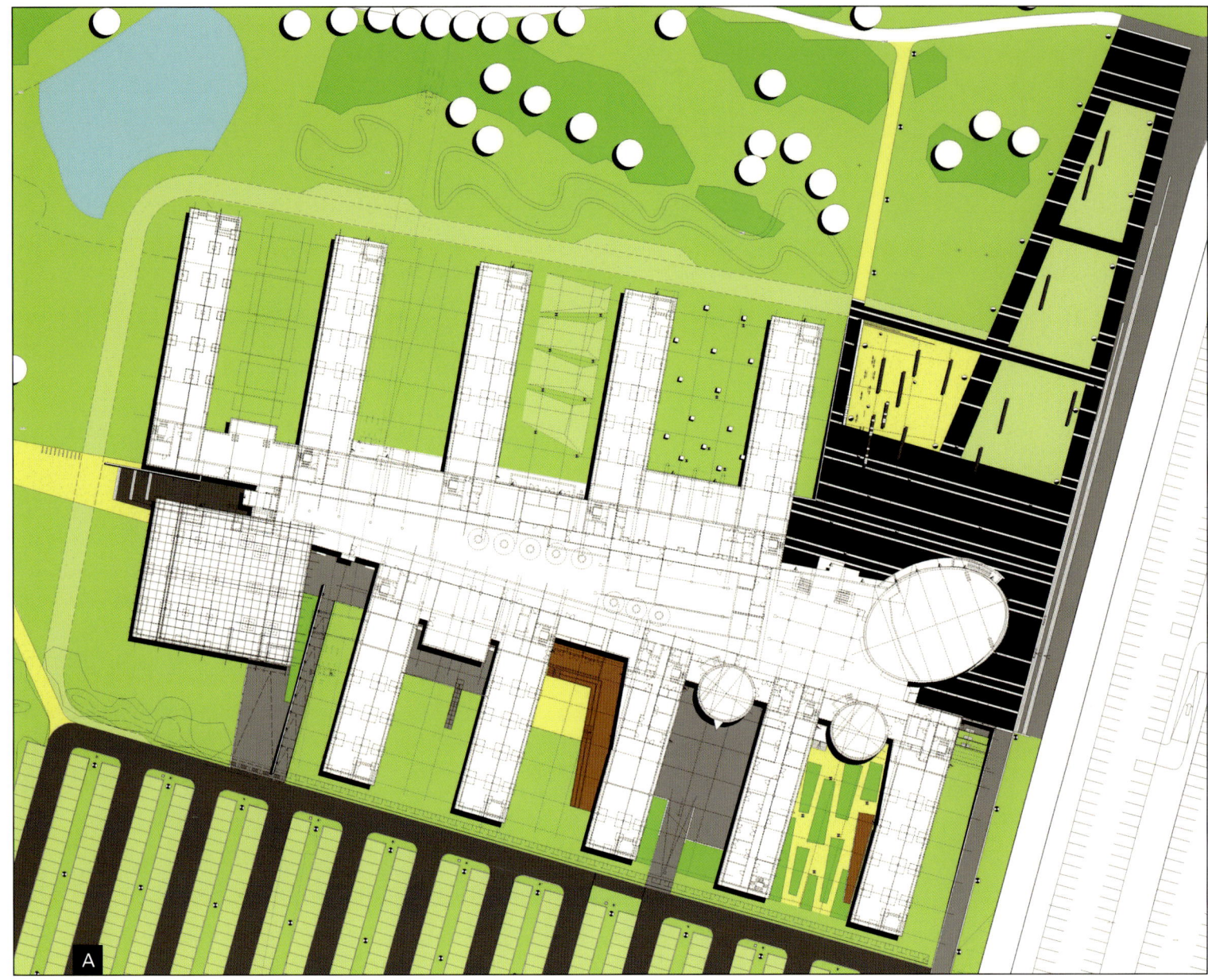

The new university-complex is connected to the central area of the campus with subway, cafeteria etc. by means of a generous forecourt. From the street and parking area, one reaches the slightly more highly lying building over a flight of steps and ramps. The central glazed hallway connects all parts of the building, and is a meeting point and area of communication, even by bad weather. The three main entrance areas come together here. The southern courtyards have a close relationship to the surrounding areas, in terms of their function and design: "Garden-yard" with plant beds and quiet benches – "large break-area" with timber-deck – "delivery yard" sunken with graphic spatial zoning – "cherry garden" with the dean's terrace. A drainage strip for surface-water closes the yard off the parking area. The entire rainwater is drained within hollows which have been creatively integrated into the overall concept. The Northern courtyard opens up to the existing green area. With its extensive design and rows of trees, connections are formed between built and "natural" space. Element from the fields of mathematics and computer science are used in abstract form to establish themes in the courtyards: Point, line, surface, form.

B

A master plan

B south entrance to the library and lobby

A

B

A	garden courtyard „bloom and leaf structure"
B	north courtyard "flower areas"
C	canteen yard

A drinking fountain made by white pigmented concrete
B break area in the schoolyard

Surrounding School House Central Grüningen

Landscape:	Dardelet GmbH, Egg ZH, Switzerland
Location:	Grüningen, Zurich, Switzerland
Client:	school administrative board of Gruningen
Completion:	2004
Size:	3.000 m^2
Costs:	800.000 CHF
Photographs:	Jean Dardelet, Oliver Bingler

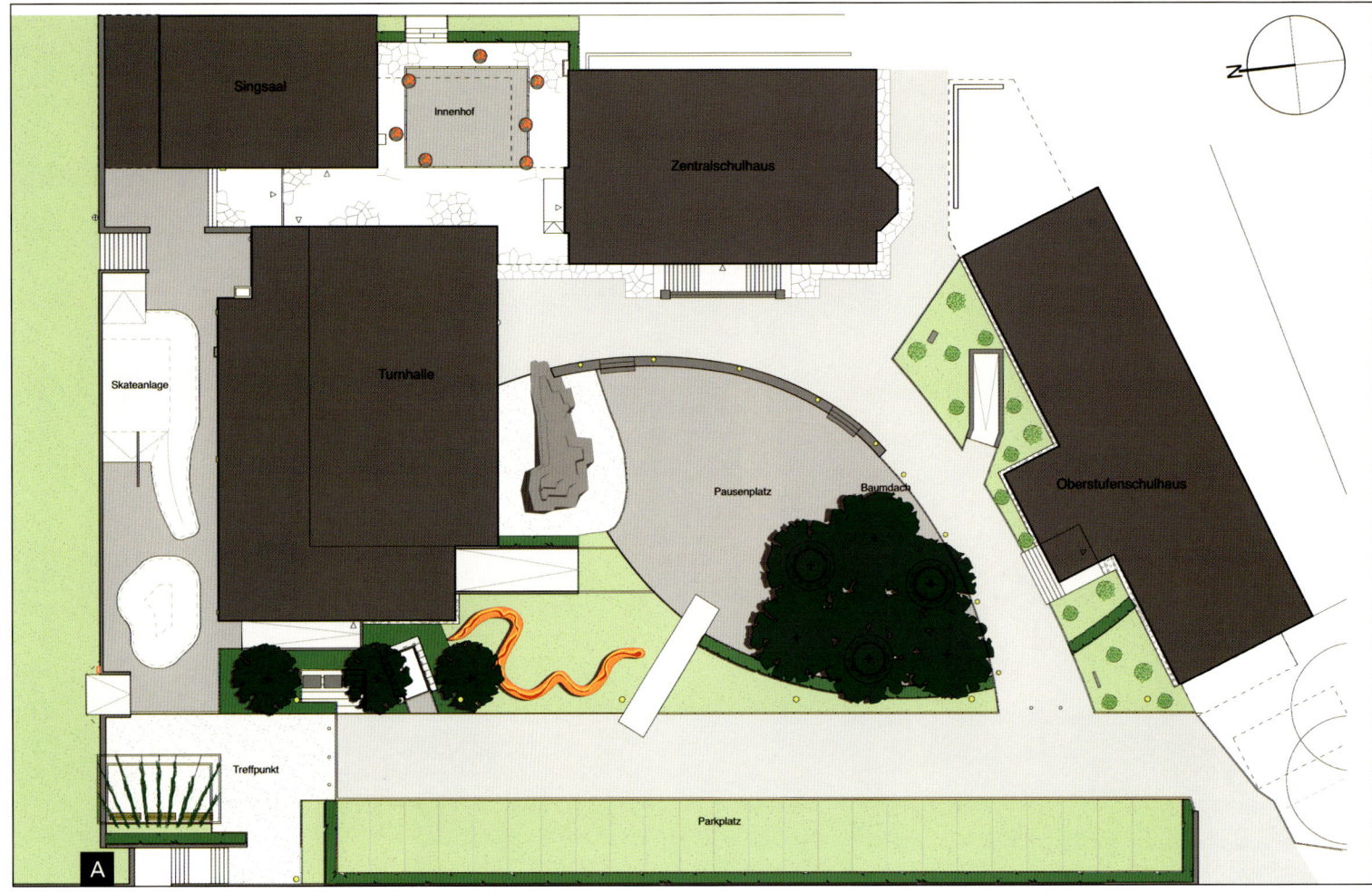

The previous playground which was covered with gravel was both car park and recreation area in one.
Furthermore it was not even ground and not at all appropriate as a schoolyard. First of all the car park has been positioned separately near to the entrance.

The problem of the uneven ground has been solved with a new seat wall which at the same time delimits the schoolyard in the form of a lens.

On one of the schoolyard trees provide schade and a fountain below them provides freshness.
On the other side an artificial rock has been placed in a particulary sunny spot. The wind-shelterd, sunny area offers beetwenn seasons a welcome sittingarea. In the schoolgrund a leasure area and an attractive skate-park has been conceived for the local youth. The inner yard was redesigned and furnished with new concrete stools.

This is their own work!
The pupils participated in the recreation of their new surroundings. They designed and produced a wall to sit on as a piece of art following the technical instructions of an artist.
The round concrete stools were designed by the landscape architect.
The children filled the surfaces with mosaics depicting chinese symbols.
Each stool is an individual work of art and has a special significance.

B

C

A master plan

B artificial rock as climbing and seat object

C subarea of the main schoolyard with round shaped benches made by chrome steel, drinking fountain and trees which will forming a future shadow roof

A

C

A	concrete stools with individual designed seating face made by pupils
B	considered recreation court with seat stools. Every class designed and build up its own stools seat face
C	mosaic snake, the mosaic covering was designed and placed-on by pupils

A

B

A lawn steps above the underground fitness area
B perennial border along the stream
C stairs leading to the tower through the sloping lawn

Guesthouse Münchener Rück

Landscape:	Valentien + Valentien
Architect:	Kiessler + Partner
Location:	Munich, Germany
Client:	Münchener Rückversicherung
Completion:	2004
Size	1200 m^2
Photographs:	Ingrid Liebald, Valentien + Valentien

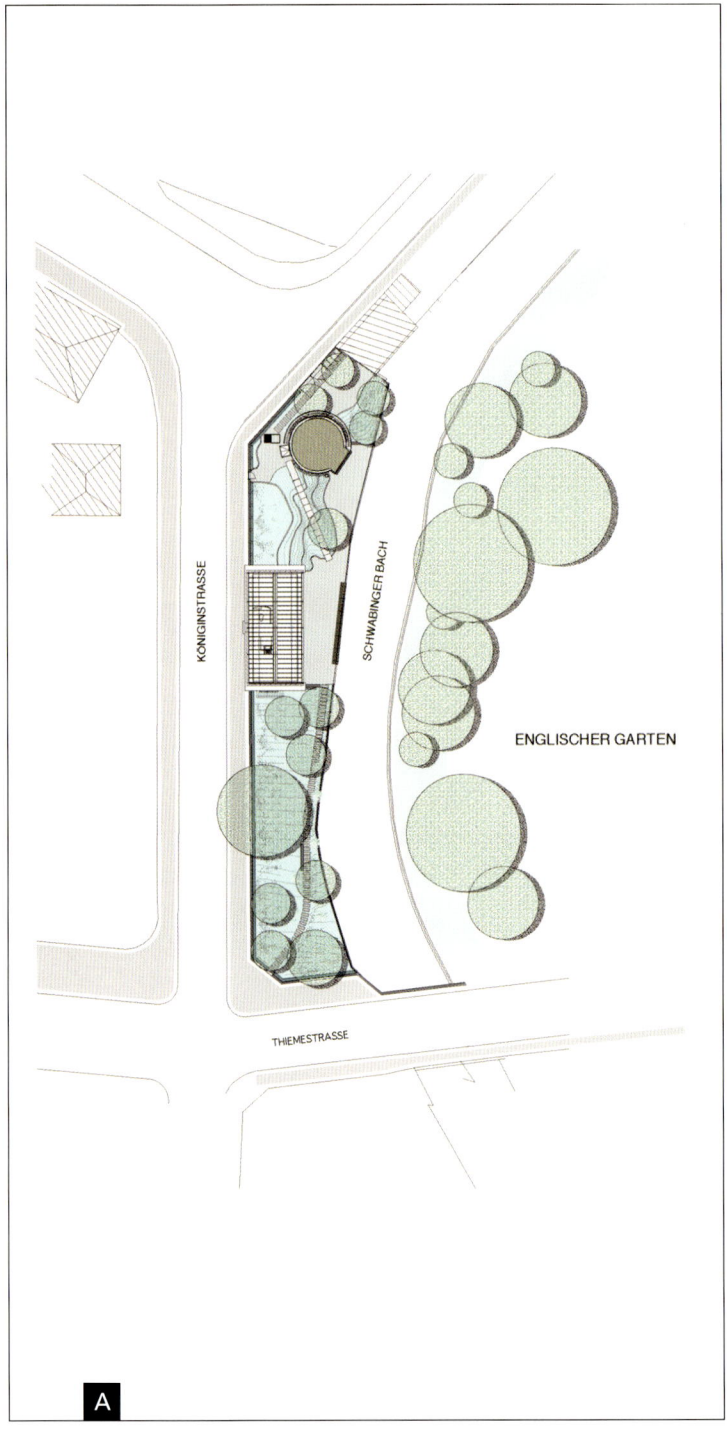

A 19th century mansion sits on the bank of the Eisbach in Munich Schwabing with a view into the English Garden. The house and garden were both in disrepair. The steep slope had run to seed, shady and damp and the bank hardly visible. The Munich reinsurance company has remodelled the mansion into a guesthouse or domicile for scholarship holders from all over the world.

The slope, situated between the remodelled mansion and a slim tower construction, was broken into distinctive layers, and a straight stairway now connects the levels. Bright pavement and the lowered retaining wall of the river lend an airier appearance to the terrace area. The result is a space in which to pause or celebrate, a space that embraces and echoes the atmosphere of the adjacent water and the English Garden.

B

C

A site plan

B terrace with polygonal flagstones

C stone bench adjacent to the garden path

A

B

C

A italian terracotta contrast green buxus cubes
B reflecting buxus
B buxus alley

Roof Garden

Landscape:	Wolfgang H. Niemeyer, Landschaftsarchitekt BDLA, DWB
Location:	München - Perlach, Germany
Client:	Privat
Completion:	2003
Size:	250 m^2
Costs:	67.000 €
Photographs:	Wolfgang H. Niemeyer

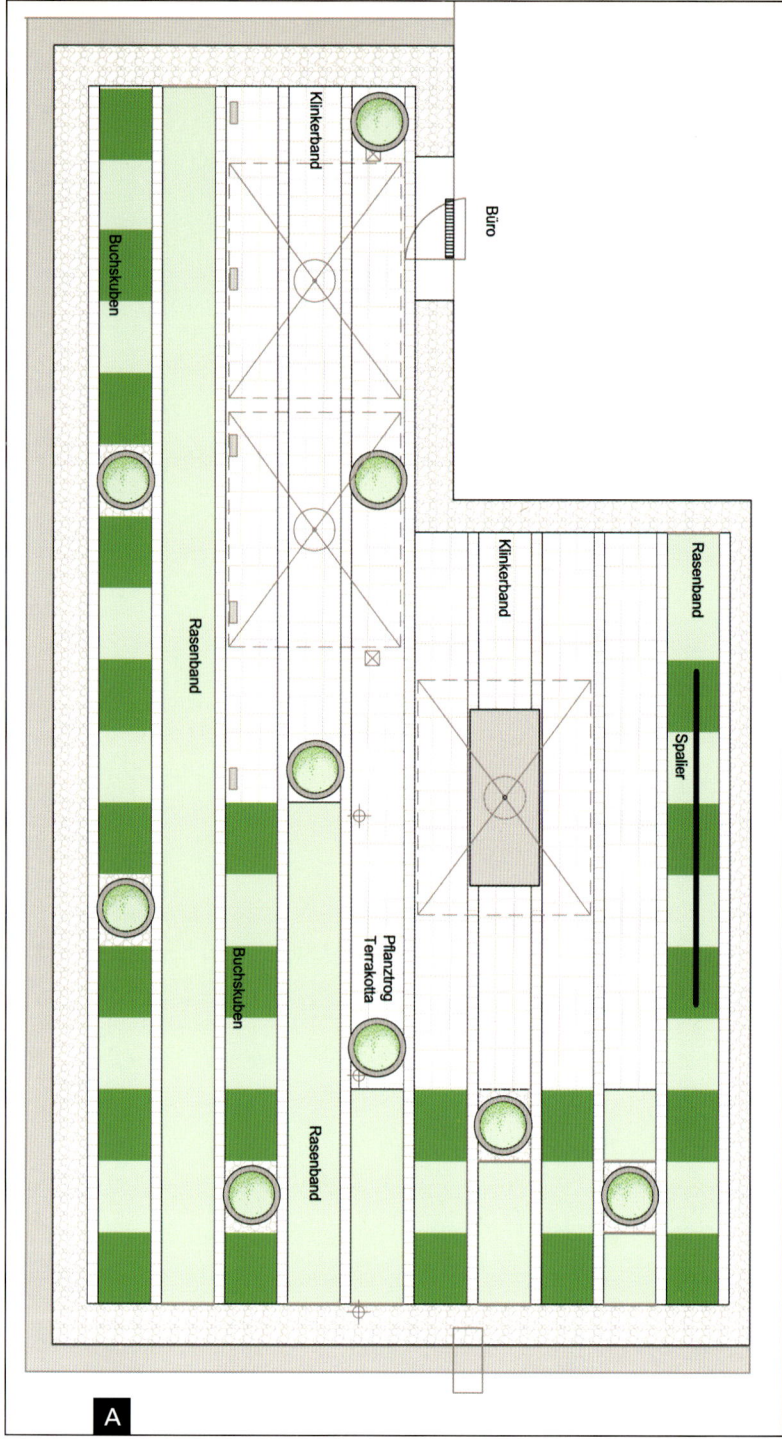

The President's "roofgarden" of a large company in Munich is a place of relaxation as well as a green oasis for summer and outdoor meetings.

Red brickstone as pavement and Italian terracotta as well as bright green of the grass stripes and dark green of buxus sempervirens characterise the garden space on the first floor of the building.

Similar to music notations, squares of buxus and terracotta solitaires function as notes between lines of brickstone and lawn stripes.

The size of the terrace is about 250 square meters. A light steel frame for the climber – clematis tangutica - and large bright parasols screen the central meeting table from the neighbourhood. Small floorlights accentuate the garden parterre at night. The gray pebble infilling of the surface drainage contrasts in colour and texture. Silent green and a moving rhythm of square and circular forms set the garden sequence to music.

B

C

A	site plan
B	music notations
C	grass stripes, brickstone stripes, light stripes

A

A adorn grass, an easy to handle plant, is the important
   structure of the design
B strong elements are connecting with the plantation to
   a elegant unit

Privat Garten Dietikon

Landscape:	planivers Landschaftsarchitekten
Location:	Dietikon, Switzerland
Client:	Privat
Completion:	2004
Size:	1000 m^2
Costs:	200.000 SFr
Photographs:	Fredy Ungricht, Jörg Zimmermann

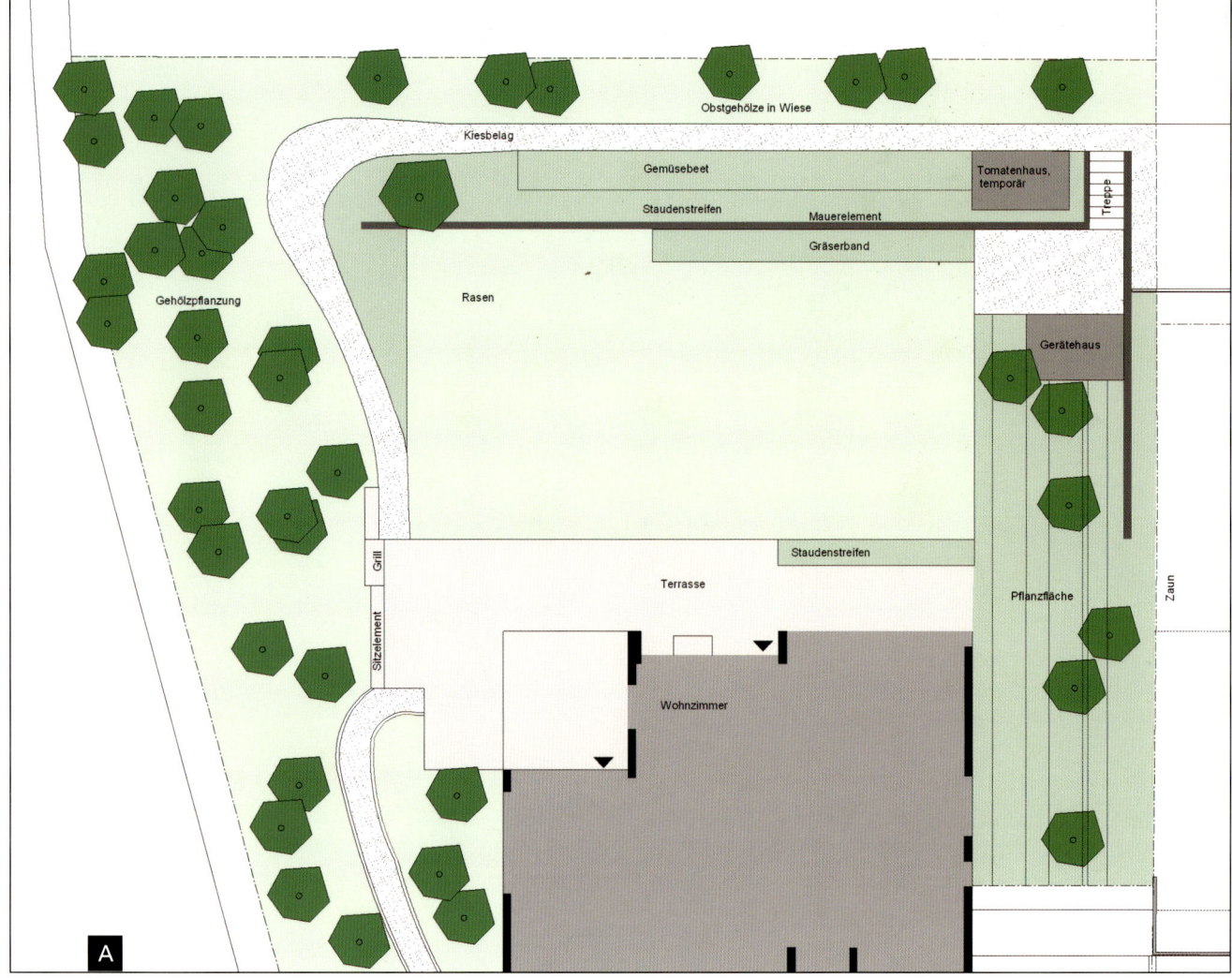

The renewing of the garden makes follow the needs of the family and gives a single family dwelling garden a modern face. The outside area near the building reflects formal-geometric form language. In the fringe areas of the garden, landscape elements like meadows and fruit trees form the bridge to the adjacent meadow landscape. With controlled range of visibility, the free landscape becomes the scenery and so a part of the garden.

The easy slop situation of the garden is caught with by terraces. Two precise shear walls offer a clearly limited, generous outside room which is perceived as an expansion of the living room. On the light concrete surfaces, leaves and blossom produce moving light reflections and shadow reflections. In the night, the light belt produces a new room feeling along the shear wall and sets new accents.

B

C

A clear geometric shapes form a nice contrast

B walls organize the garden structure

C plants and concrete elements get strengthen

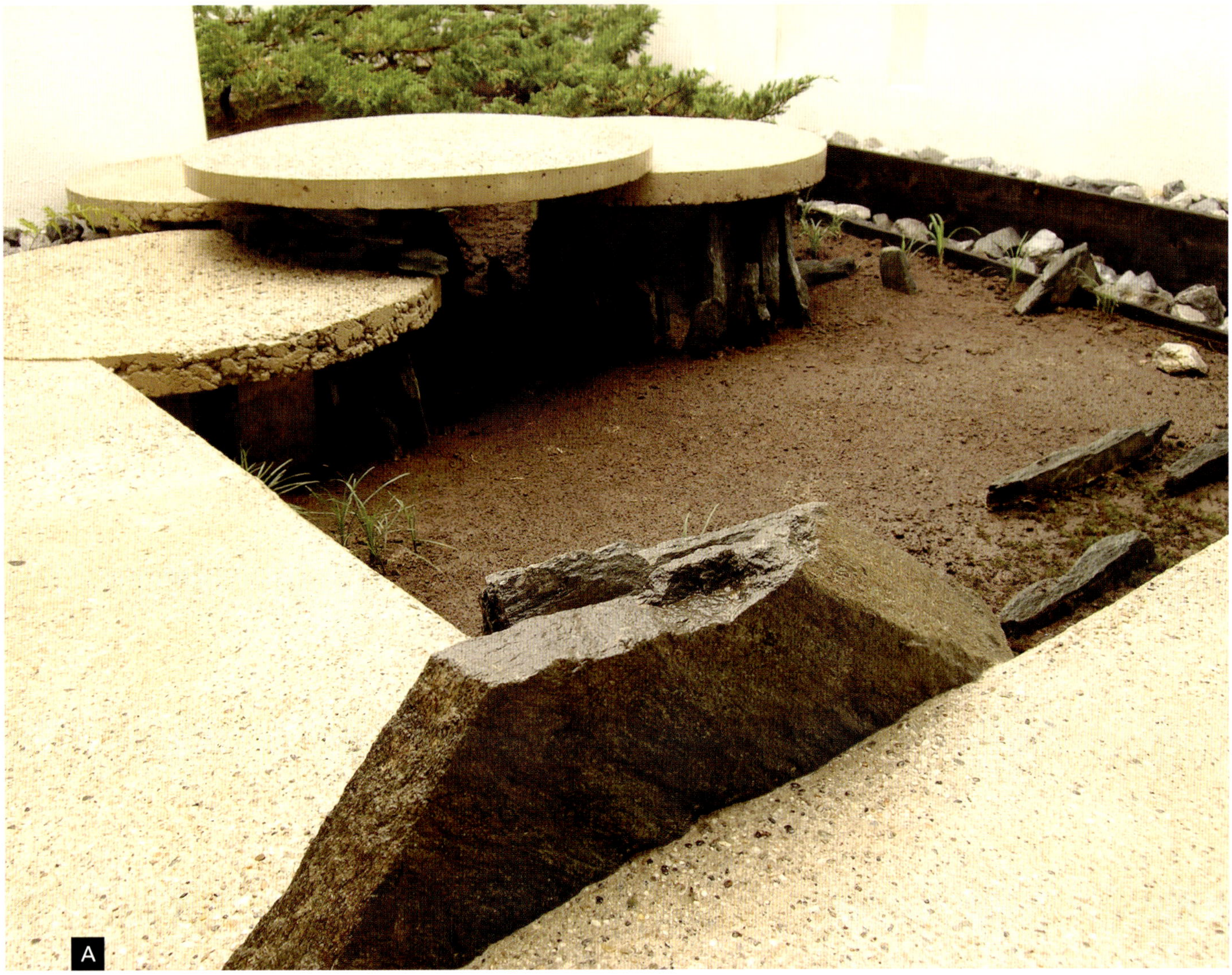

A

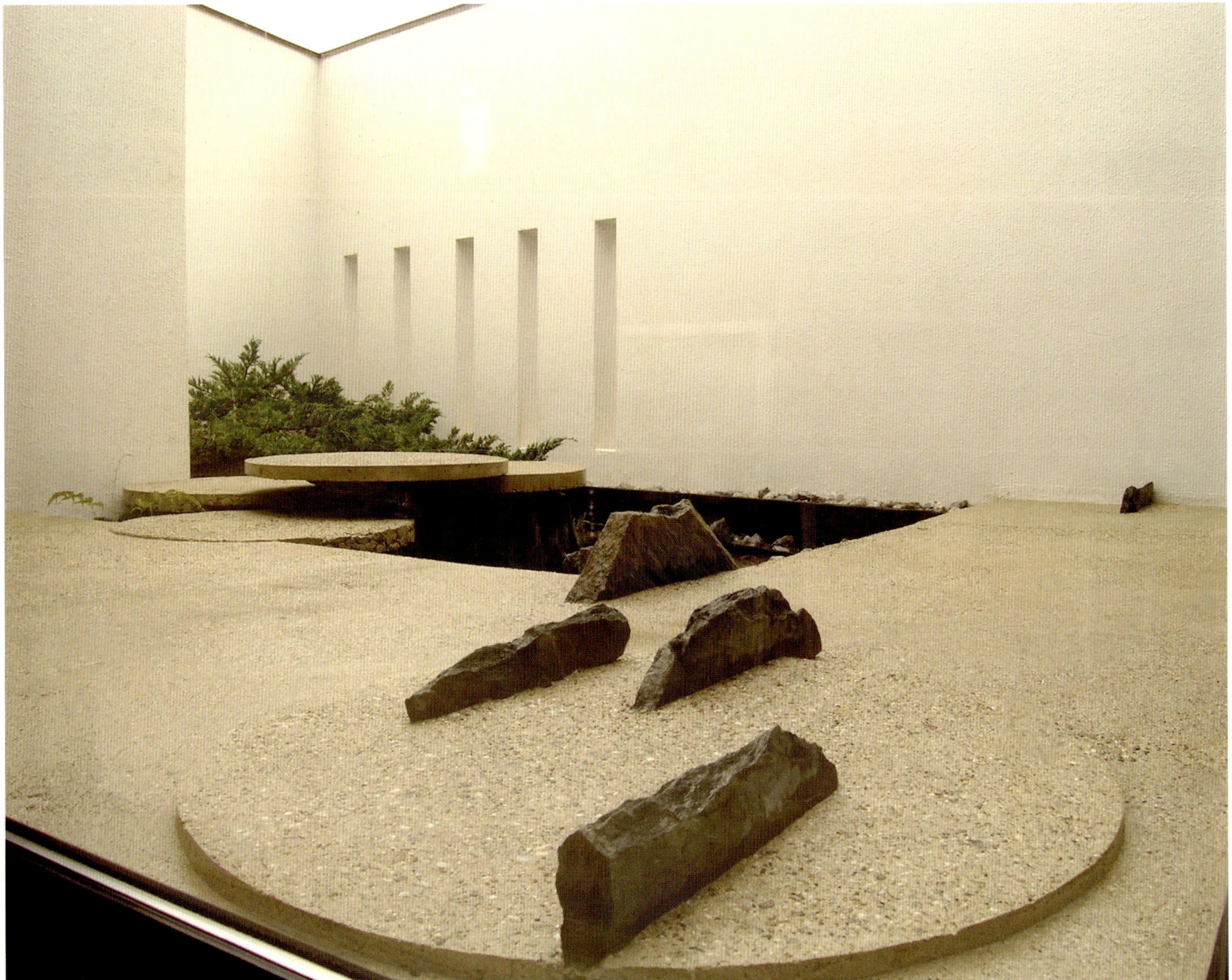

B

C

A view of the setting of garden rocks
B view from Dining room
C 4 undirection objects

The Garden without the direction

Landscape:	N-tree / Takeshi Nagasaki
Location:	Nishimagome Oota-ku, Tokyo
Client:	Privat
Completion:	2006
Size:	22 m²
Photographs:	Takeshi Nagasaki

深草洗い出し80%

自然石 平板

王.石ケ利

A

This garden is in the courtyard of a good view from the living of the residence. I crossed the round object of the five-ring / 5 body with the same line as a floor level. The point of the viewpoint is the cavern under a round object. It has been done setting of garden rocks with a small blue stone into the cavern,
I planted low Juniperus Chinese var. procumbens, without planting the high tree of the back to lower the viewpoint. I am showing same time the dark complicated world of the bright simple scenery and under of the top on the basis of a gland level.

There is nothing in the round object in this time, although design bamboo to the work of a round object until now and was indicating the direction.

The circle that there is not the direction means infinity. In other words the garden without the direction is an infinite garden.

A first planning

B view from second floor

C view from Living room

GREEN BELT

Modern Landscape Design

INDEX

asp Landschaftsarchitekten AG

Tobeleggweg 19, 8049 Zürich
T +44 34 16 16 1 / F +44 34 10 14 9
www.aspland.ch
info@aspland.ch

Asp leaves marks – once asp leaves clearly visible accents of cultural creations and design punctuation, another time hardly visually noticeably as an expression of the preserving or new creations of value living space.

The individuality of the respective place, its history, the future and ecology demand for every task an unambiguous answer if qualities should remain, promoted or new accents are supposed to be set.

Creative solutions will emerge out of the presentation of desirable ideal and the knowledge of the real context.

City, country and environment are the space in which asp plans are constructs and formed. Based on interdisciplinary collaboration and long-time experience sustainable projects became develop as an answer on complex questions in city planning, landscape architecture and environment planning.

B . A . E . R .
BECSEI + HACKENBRACHT

Spitzenstrasse 2, 60437 Frankfurt am Main
T +49 61 01 40 37 60 / F +49 61 01 40 37 62
www.b-a-e-r.com
mail@b-a-e-r.com

Stephan Becsei (*1957) and Christine Hackenbracht (*1955), both graduates of Kassel Combined Polytechnic and University, founded their own practice in 1989. It has the following philosophy: "To confront the site with integrated, resolute forms and clear concepts. Transience is beginning now – nature will claw everything back." Their work covers city squares, pedestrian zones, rainwater management, lighting concepts and lighting design.

BÜRO KIEFER
Landscape architect Ms. Prof. Dipl. Ing. Gabriele G. Kiefer

Mariannenplatz 23   10997 Berlin – Kreuzberg
T +49 30 61 70 98 70 +49 30 61 70 98 03 / F +49 30 61 70 98 05
www.buero-kiefer.de
info@buero-kiefer.de

BÜRO KIEFER became establish in 1989 as landscape architecture office of Gabriele G. Kiefer. At present the office has 15 employees. The main working field are landscape architectural realizations and design work. The type, character and dimension of the projects cover a large spectrum. Public municipal places and parks belong to the work of BÜRO KIEFER as well as residential areas, commercial areas, kindergartens, schools and up to roof gardens. In the last years BÜRO KIEFER was active planning at large city parks next to a series of projects for conversion locations.

The design philosophy of BÜRO KIEFER is based on the idea "free space is a last sphere in the world" which let space for creativity of a "counter design" according to the current situation of globalization, mobility and information technology.

As a sequence of this view, the design idea of BÜRO KIEFER is essentially constructed on the terms of clarity, reduction as well as a (transformed) reference to the existing environment. Perceptible room becomes therewith the main characteristic of the design.

Dardelet GmbH
Büro für Landschaftsarchitektur

Gewerbestrasse 12, 8132 Egg ZH, Switzerland
T +41 44 98 43 30 3 / F +41 44 98 40 95 0
www.dardelet.ch
info@dardelet.ch

owner: Jean Dardelet, Landscape Architect SIA BSLA
employees: 2-3
founded: 1989
categorys:
open space design and planning
landscape design and planning
landscape managing
golf course design and planning
environmental services and planning
consulting services
jury works (competitions board)
categories including:
feasibility studies, master plans and reports, concept designs, residential designs, planting plans, environmental compatibility reports, vegetation management, water sensitive design, eco resort planning)

DS Landschapsarchitecten (Maike van Stiphout, Jana Crepon) & NL architects (Kamiel Klaasse)

GTL Gnüchtel - Triebswetter Landscape architects

DS Landschapsarchitecten
Overtoom 197, 1054 HT Amsterdam
T +31 20-5301252 F +31 20-4230627
info@ds.landschapsarchitecten.nl
www.ds.landschapsarchitecten.nl

NL Architects
Van Hallstraat 294, NL 1051 HM Amsterdam
T +31 20 62 07 32 3   F +31 20 63 86 19 2
www.nlarchitects.nl
E_office@nlarchitects.nl

Grüner Weg 21, 34117 Kassel, Germany
T +49 56 17 89 46 10 / F +49 56 17 89 46 11
kontakt@gtl-kassel.de
www.gtl-kassel.de

DS is an office for landscape architecture with wide reaching experience, gained through a large number of projects, from strategic planning to precise solutions for design tasks. In the Netherlands DS belongs to the core of renowned offices for landscape architecture. "Continuity" is an important term in landscape. Each design takes form as the newest layer of time. Knowledge and experience are necessary to interpret the past and to translate them into the future. We therefore have a strong network of advisors out of the field of the ecology, hydrology and geology.

DS loves the "homo ludens", the playful people who prefer stimulating surroundings above a space that dictates its own use.

NL Architects is an Amsterdam based office. The initial four principals, Pieter Bannenberg, Walter van Dijk, Kamiel Klaasse and Mark Linnemann, officially opened practice in January 1997, but had shared workspace already since the early nineties. All were educated at Delft University. Their projects often focus on ordinary aspects of everyday life, including the unappreciated or negative, that are enhanced or twisted in order to bring to the fore the unexpected potential of the things that surround us.

Markus Gnüchtel and Michael Triebswetter founded GTL Gnüchtel -Triebswetter landscape architects in 1991 in Kassel, the city of the world famous nature park, the upland called Wilhelmshöhe. In 2000 the opening of a further office location followed in Munich. GTL is active in China, where there is, starting 2005, a shared Peking office with Rainer Schmidt landscape architects.

The owners' credo: to realize innovative designs with best possible perfection in detailed planning and project management. Participating in numerous competitions – usually announced as pan-European competitions – gives the practice the opportunity to constantly break new grounds in conceptual thinking, and in the final realisation and presentation of their design ideas. More than 30 first prizes in competitions, e.g. the internationally highly recognized first award for Manhattan´s Pier 40 (together with tec architecture, Los Angeles), and several national and international Landscape Design Awards reflect GTL´s constant thrive for best possible result.

GORA art&landscape

GUSTAFSON PORTER Ltd.

Vilebov. 4a, SE-217 63 MALMO, SWEDEN
T +46 40 91 19 13 / F +46 40 91 19 03
www.gora.se
info@gora.se

Linton House 39-51, Highgate Road London NW5 1RS
T +44 20 72 67 20 05 / F +44 20 74 85 92 03
www.gustafson-porter.com
enquiries@ gustafson-porter.com

Monika Gora, born in 1959, has been working as a landscape architect and artist with her own office, GORA art&landscape, since 1989. She holds a master's degree in landscaping from the Swedish University of Agriculture. Before starting her own office Monika Gora made prolonged travels of work and study in Australia, China, Indonesia, the Netherlands, New Zealand and the USA. She is a member of the Swedish National Council for Architecture, Form and Design. In her practice she has systematically chosen her own paths – both experimenting and challenging – combining this with an ability to find practicable solutions.

Gustafson Porter is based in London and has projects in Britain, Europe, the Middle East and Asia. Gustafson Porter operates across the diverse disciplines of landscape, architecture, engineering and design. Their work expresses the tension and balance between opposing forces in the built and natural worlds in a striking and contemporary manner. Gustafson Porter's work is inspired by the complexity of the human condition and the desire for stability as well as change in the modern world. The approach is simultaneously rational and emotional, disciplined but loose, structured yet ever changing.

The practice has three directors; landscape architect/artist Kathryn Gustafson and architects Neil Porter and Mary Bowman. Together with the other members of the office they provide a diverse range of expertise within the fields of landscape, architecture and urban design.

HÄFNER/JIMENEZ

Schwedter Straße 263 D-10119 Berlin
T + 49 30 28 39 13 03 / F + 49 30 28 39 13 12
www.haefner-jimenez.de
info@haefner-jimenez.de

TRADITION AND FUTURE

It is not our intention to quote the history of building and landscape art or to resurrect it. We work in the controlled context of contemporary and future challenges. Historical precedents are not used as references to past times, but are investigated for their functional principals. In the presence of design, this is what gives definition and proportion to the future of the space.

BUILDING ECONOMICALLY

Our aim is to create spaces of high value using the simple strategy of introducing some elements of higher quality onto inexpensive surfaces. Our guiding principal is to create complex spaces with simple resources.

THE WATERFRONT

Water positions are desired locations. Our office has made itself famous by planning and constructing projects on the waterfront. Planning and building on the waterfront means creating an environment with spaces for contemplating the water and the life on the opposite bank.

HUBERT WENDLER LANDSCHAFTSARCHITEKT BDLA

Pfeuferstrasse 38, 81373 München
T +49 89 46 13 97 0 / F +49 89 46 13 97 29
www.fine-gardens.de
wendler@p-38.de

The architecture firm was founded in 1985 by Hubert Wendler. Since then we develop successfully projects of all sizes and types in the range of landscape architecture such as gardens, parks and green areas around housings, educational institutions, offices and so forth. The individual tasks in these projects are worked out with a lot of creativity and affection for detail. During the whole planning process we attach high importance to innovative an economic solutions.

HUTTERREIMANN + CEJKA Landschaftsarchitektur

Möckernstraße 68, 10965 Berlin
F +49 30 78 89 88 25 / F +49 30 78 09 54 88
www.hr-c.net
hutterreimann@hr-c.net

Foundation:
Cejka Landschaftsarchitektur 1993 in Vienna
hutterreimann Landschaftsarchitektur 2001 in Berlin
Collaboration as hutterreimann + cejka Landschaftsarchitektur since 2001
Fields of activity:
Landscape architecture, urban and rural development
Building typology:
Parks, squares, garden festivals, privat gardens, sports- and leisure-grounds, playgrounds
Project partners:
Collaboration with renowned architects and specialist consultants
Corporate philosophy:
On a solid foundation of experience and pragmatism we are looking for unusual, experimental and futuristic solutions. Efficiency, quality management and flexibility are the base of collaboration with our project partners. In our work conventional and new ideas, reflection and pictorial poetry melt into one another

JOHANNES GROTHAUS LANDSCHAFTSARCHITEKTEN STADTPLANER | BDLA

Gregor-Mendel-Strasse 36/37, 14469 Potsdam, Germany
T +49 331 749 84-0 / F +49 331 749 84-99
www.johannesgrothaus.de
info@johannesgrothaus.de

Philosophie

The harmony between man and environment city and landscape needs a critical mind, which considers the history of the places, the natural resources and the new requirements. This happens under the premise of: Registering special qualities of the place Defining requirements and planning intentions and transforming them into a contemporary and functional form Showing the tensions in the relationship between city and landscape Seeing the public and private open space as a central aspect of urban planning and Landscape architecture as well as an important design task for our environment.

Koepfli Partner GmbH Landschaftsarchitekten BSLA

Neustadtstrasse 3 6003 Luzern
T +41 22 61 64 6 / F +41 22 61 62 7
www.koepflipartner.ch
buero@koepflipartner.ch

Stefan Koepfli, born 1961 in Lucerne, studied from 1986 - 1990 landscape architecture at the Technical University Rapperswil. Stefan Koepfli has been leading his own office since 1994, and has won in this period several national and international competitions and realised over 80 projects. Permanent collaborators since 2001: Jeannette Rinderknecht and Blanche Keeris

KuhnTruninger Landschaftsarchitekten GmbH

Ankerstrasse 3, CH-8004 Zürich
T +41 44 291 18 19 / F +41 44 291 18 20
www.kuhntruninger.ch
mail@kuhntruninger.ch

The work of KuhnTruninger landscape architects is seeking after a specially expression of a location, with the objective on creating coherent and at the same time usable open spaces.

Specific by avoiding uniform shapes and at the same time common by using everyday materials.

landschaftDrei
ingenieure + landschaftsarchitekten

Pforzheimer Strasse 262, 70499 Stuttgart
T +49 71 16 93 49 66 / F +49 71 16 93 49 64
www.landschaftDrei.de
info (at) landschaftDrei.de

Our team consists of landscape architects, engineers and an alternating pool of interns. Moreover, we cooperate with city, traffic and light planners as well as media engineers, communication designers, geographers, ecologists and artists. Depending on the demands of the specific project, we build working partnerships with studios from Germany, Europe or Australia.
Our Values
We embrace an interdisciplinary, integrated approach to all of our projects. From the very beginning of a project each discipline should be involved in finding an optimal solution for our client. In order to build a powerful working team, we actively engage in intensive communication and an exchange of ideas with the persons we work with. The more enthusiasm and joy the members of our working team develop, the more smoothly and dynamic our projects will be realized. Our aim is to always organize the planning process in a way which is optimal to all parties involved. We are convinced that cross-cultural cooperations call for a reciprocal understanding of the working processes of each party involved in the project.

LATZ+PARTNER Landscape Architecture

Ampertshausen 6 D - 85402 Kranzberg
T +49 81 66 67 85 0 / F +49 81 66 67 85 33
www.latzundpartner.de
post@latzundpartner.de

1968 founded in Aachen and Saarbrücken, the office was
transferred to Kassel in 1974 and into the region of Munich in 1988.
Project offices in Duisburg since 1999, since 2001 in Bremerhaven and since 2006 in London together with Meadowcroft Griffin Architects.
The office is working on an international scale.
Realized plannings contain projects of town-planning and urban design as well as large-scale landscape architecture, planning of open space and ecological building up to research work in the field of alternative technologies, connected with the achievement of long-term development and maintenance programs.
The office stands not only for quality of design but also for technical com-petence and know-how. Since the mid eighties a focus of the work is dealing with the metamorphosis of postindustrial sites.
Dependent on the type of the project, the office has working - teams with partner - offices and specialists.

LEVIN MONSIGNY LANDSCHAFTSARCHITEKTEN GmbH

LEX-KERFERS LANDSCHAFTSARCHITEKTEN

The Bridge 8 Room 2206 8-10 Jian Guo Zhong Rd
PRC - 200025 Shanghai
T +86 21 64 45 05 19 / F +86 21 64 45 05 39

Brunnenstraße 181 D - 10119 Berlin
T +49 30 44053184 / F +49 30 44053175
www.levin-monsigny.com
shanghai@levin-monsigny.com

Levin Monsigny Landscape Architects is an international landscape design firm based in Berlin. We offer a full range of landscaping and urban design and have carried out commissions for public plazas and parks, mixed-use developments, residential estates, private and historical gardens.

Our highly-experienced team is united by its passion for discovering new places, for contributing to a more liveable environment and by the challenge of finding individual solutions to match people's needs. The unusual results have the stamp of an unmistakable identity of place.

Over the years the firm has joined forces with renowned architects in creating outstanding projects and has won many prestigious design competitions, such as the Museum Island in Berlin, a World Cultural Heritage Site.

For the past few years we have successfully developed our activity in China with a variety of projects in Shanghai, Hangzhou, Ningbo and Dalian.

Emling 25, 85461 Bockhorn, Germany
T +49 81 22 94 38 01   +49 81 22 94 38 02
www.lex-kerfers.de
mail@lex-kerfers.de

The practice was founded in 1998 by Rita Lex-Kerfers and has been managed since 1993 in partnership with Robert Kerfers. They regard landscape architecture - particularly construction work for public space – as an expression of how to deal with specific situations, the context of the site, and – not least – the function required. Based on this approach, interdisciplinary collaboration is a major aspect of their way of working.

N-TREE   TAKESHI NAGASAKI

planivers Landschaftsarchitekten AG

2-13-2 Nishibori, Niiza-shi Saitama 352-0031 Japan
T +81 90 80 45 46 59
http://www.n-tree.jp
nagasaki@n-tree.jp

Nagasaki is a landscape gardener and an artist who creates 'space of encounter'. Gardens are unique spaces where so many elements are encounter such as buildings & grounds, clients, architects & gardeners, products & nature, old & new, lights & shadows and west & east. Nagasaki applies different media to express those encounters beyond categories of arts, design, sculpture and garden.

1970	Born in Nara, Japan
1990	Studied Tokyo National University of Fine Arts and Music
1990-91	Studied Oil painting at Universidad Complutense de Madrid in Spain
	Visited the American Reservation of the South Dakota Tribe in 1991, 92, 94
1992	After Returning from Spain, Started Woodcut Printing and Sculpture
1995	After Graduation, Independent Learning of Landscape
1997	Established N-tree (the Heart of Tree, Heart of Man, Heart of Garden)

Birmensdorferstrasse 55, 8004 Zürich, Schweiz
T +41 44 24 54 60 7 / F +41 44 24 54 60 5
www.planivers.ch
ungricht@planivers.ch

The planivers landscape architects CORP. plans and designs public and private space for urban and settlements areas: Commercial and industry areas, sport and leisure space, areas for retired person and residential areas, upgrading of landscape.

Our projects are based on the atmospheric character of the relevant place. We realize sustainable projects and strive to a high design standard. The professional organizing of the projects, the keeping of the schedule and the costs aware management are obvious for us.

Operating and supporting of the project is for us already important in early planning phases. Therefore maintenance concepts are one our core competency. The realized projects can be developing further with its users.

CEO and owner of the planivers: Fredy Ungricht, Landschaftsarchitekt dipl. Ing. FH

Photographer of the portrait of F. Ungricht is © Olivia Heussler, Zürich

Planungsbüro Drecker

Bottroper Strasse 6, 46244 Bottrop-Kirchhellen (Germany)
T +49 20 45 95 61-0 / F +49 20 45-9561-24
www.drecker.de
bottrop@drecker.de

History
The office was founded 1982 in Hannover (Niedersachsen, Germany). The original field of activity - project and object design - was soon completed by nationwide tasks of landscape planning and environmental concepts. This expansion of tasks required the establishment of a new location in Bottrop- Kirchhellen (Nordrhein-Westfalen, Germany) in 1985. Because of the reinforcement of activities in the new federal states of East Germany since 1992, it became necessary to establish new branches of Planungs-büro Drecker in Potsdam (Brandenburg, Germany) and Halle (Sachsen-Anhalt, Germany).

PROAP - Estudos e Projectos de Arquitectura Paisagista, Lda

Rua Dom Luis I, 19 - 6º, 1200-149 LISBOA – PORTUGAL
T +35 12 13 95 17 24 / F +35 12 13 95 35 20
www.proap.pt
proap@proap.pt

PROAP, Lda. is a Landscape Architecture Project and Planning Partnership that was founded in 1989, in Lisbon. Its activity falls mainly upon the following fields:
- project;
- landscape planning;
- environmental evaluation;
- project/construction control;
- urban project and planning.
PROAP gathers a wide group of landscape architects, architects, designers, plastic artists, who are represented by João Nunes and Carlos Ribas. The work and research intentions of the studio have been mainly oriented according to a principle of intervention in landscape that recognizes its rules and functional mechanisms.
In 2001-2002 PROAP travels around Italy with an exhibition, shown in Milano, Modena, Torino, Benevento, Salerno, Venezia and Roma, selected to represent Portugal at the 8th "Biennale di Architettura di Venezia", which assembles some of its most representative projects.

RAINER SCHMIDT LANDSCHAFTSARCHITEKTEN

Klenzestrasse 57c - 80469 München
T +49 89 20 25 35 0 / F +49 89 20 25 35 30
www.rainerschmidt.com
info@rainerschmidt.com

With over 20 years of professional work experience as a landscape designer Prof. Rainer Schmidt has one of the largest and most well-known offices in Germany. There are a lot of projects on different scales realized in Germany. The office has about 30 staff members including senior landscape architects, landscape architects, graphic designers and administrators. There are three locations of the office in Germany: The main office is in Munich and there are also offices in Berlin and in Bernburg. At the same time Prof. Schmidt is a professor at the University of Applied Sciences in Berlin and adjunct professor at Peking University. The working fields of the office are the planning and execution of large projects in the fields of landscape architecture, environmental planning, urban design and supervision on both national and international level. The office´s aim is to find ways of dealing with problems of our time. The language of landscape architecture in the 21st century must offer a realistic reflection of the way people interact with each other and with nature. The office is striving to achieve a balance between design, function, emotion and conservation. Rainer Schmidt established an shared office with GTL Landscapearchitects in Bejing, China in March 2005 and have been doing many large scale projects in China during the past two years like the design for the Olympic Park in Beijing, Software Park in Dalian and Cixi Rivershore Design.

relais Landschaftsarchitekten

Rosenheimer Straße 7, 10781 Berlin
T +49 30 23 62 97 21 / F +49 30 23 62 97 22
www.relaisLA.de
buero@relaisLA.de

Landscape architecture is always a fascinating challenge. Coming from the needs of the users, the spatial facts as well as the history of the place we'll develop an individual concept for each situation. Openly and curiously we search with every task for the correct questions and design future prospective and correct answers.
The spectrum of work reaches from urban to the scenic context, from urban structural scale to the concrete object. At the same time we understand ourselves explicitly as experts for landscape architecture, that solve complex task positions in the team with architects, engineers and advisers.

ST raum a.   landscape architecture

Waldemarstrasse 33,10999 Berlin
T +49 30 61 66 09 0 / F +49 30 61 66 09 17
www.strauma.com
info@strauma.com

Established in 1991 by landscape architects Stefan Jäckel and Tobias Micke, our office has completed numerous German and international projects for urban squares and other inner city open spaces including, office and commercial properties, hotels, community centres and residential environments. Urban design studies and master plans supplement our range of services. Our office for landscape architecture plans open spaces where people can feel comfortable and enjoy their vitality. We ask what stimulates people, what wishes they have and what they need. Conscious selection of materials and the arrangement of individual elements make our projects useable for today and the future.
In business for over a decade, our team of up to 15 highly motivated and experienced professionals work in close collaboration with planning partners and manage the projects. Our comprehensive, interdisciplinary network of consultants ensures optimal solutions for specialised situations. Our success in meeting time schedules and budgets is proven through several realised projects.

TOPOTEK1

Sophienstraße 18, 10178 Berlin
T +49 30 24 62 58 - 00 / F +49 30 24 62 58 - 99
www.topotek1.de
topotek1@topotek1.de

The task central to our office is the design of urban open spaces. Based on a critical understanding of immanent realities, the search for conceptual approaches leads us to decided statements concerning the urban context. Throughout design, planning, and construction we offer solutions for independent new parks, squares, sports-grounds, courtyards and gardens, whose designs answer to contemporary requirements for variability, communication and sensuality. The manifold experiences through a broad spectrum of German and international projects meanwhile capacitate an efficient realization, finely tuned to respective necessities.
Partners:
Martin Rein-Cano was born in Buenos Aires in 1967. After studying landscape architecture at the university of Hannover, he worked from 1994 to 1996 at the office Buero Kiefer. In 1996 he founded the office TOPOTEK 1 in Berlin.
Lorenz Dexler was born in Darmstadt in 1968. After studying landscape architecture at the university of Hannover, he worked in partnership with TOPOTEK 1. Since 1999 he is the partner of Martin Rein-Cano.

Valentien + Valentien
Landscape Architects and City Planners SRL
Prof. Christoph Valentien, Prof. Donata Valentien

Hauptstrasse 42, 82234 Wessling, Germany
T +49 81 53 95 20 10 / F +49 81 53 95 20 14
www.valentien.de
valentien@valentien.de

Founded in Stuttgart in 1971
From 1982 on in Weßling/ Bavaria
Projects:
Consulting and Planning:
design and construction planning
landscape planning
urban planning
ecological and urbanistic surveys
Equipment:
network with 7 Macs and 1 PC
laser printer, color printer, plotter

WEIDINGER LANDSCHAFTSARCHITEKTEN

Wilhelmstraße 118 D – 10963 Berlin
T +49 30 288 86 48 - 0 / F +49 30 288 86 48 - 99
www.weidingerlandschaftsarchitekten.de
post@weidingerlandschaftsarchitekten.de

Performances
landscape design: gardens, courtyards, squares, parks, streets, greenbelts, traffic planning and civil engineering
Vita Weidinger
assistant professor at TU Berlin, 1993 - 1998
assistant professor at ENSP, Versailles, France, 1999-2000
guest professor at BerTU Berlin, 2004 - 2006
publications and lectures
2002 German urban planning price for green belt, Großenhain
Selected projects
outdoor facilities law faculty, University Frankfurt, 2005, 1. prize and realization
outdoor facilities Jessop Hospital University of Sheffield, England, 2005, realization
Nöldner sqaure, Berlin, 2004 - 2007, 1. prize and realization
railway station Barmbek, Hamburg, 2005 - 2009, 1. prize and realization

WES & Partner
Wehberg Schatz Betz Kaschke
Landscape architects

Jarrestrasse 80, 22303 Hamburg
T +49 40 27 84 1-0 / F +49 40 27 06 66 8
www.wesup.de
wesup@wesup.de

Wolfgang H. Niemeyer
Landschaftsarchitekten BDLA DWB

80687 München, Agnes-Bernauer Platz 8
T +49 89 58 79 89 / F +49 89 58 74 48
WolfgangNiemeyer@t-online.de

The work of our office WES & Partner includes the design of the architectural interior- and outdoor spaces: open space- and object planning, urban green space- and landscape planning, expert reports and urban projects, as well as art in public spaces.

We place a great deal of importance on all of the working phases, imposing high standards regarding content, "artistic" quality, and professional realisation.

WES & Partner have completed several projects as master planners, including the International Horticultural Show 2003 in Rostock, the redesign of the Jungfernstieg in Hamburg, and the station surroundings in Erfurt.

We are also active internationally, working on expert's reports and competitions from Moscow to Shanghai. In Utrecht we are presently working on the area surrounding the Dutch Ministry of Transport and in Salzburg on the extension of the Faculty for Humanities and Cultural Sciences.

In Spring 2006 we were awarded the 1st prize in the international competition "Länsisatamanpuisto Jewel" in Helsinki.

We have also been working on realising large-scale projects in China for more than eight years.

Less is more – creative landscape architecture as it relates to architecture" is the guiding concept of this landscapearchitecture practice, founded in 1985. Wolfgang Niemeyer is also engaged in widening the concepts of his disciplin: thus language, and particularly music, in the form of sound arrangements and sound installatios in open spaces, are becoming a constituent part of landscape architecture.

GREEN BELT: MODERN LANDSCAPE DESIGN

Copyright © 2007 by Liaoning Science and Technology Press

Published in 2007 by
Page One Publishing Private Limited
20 Kaki Bukit View
Kaki Bukit Techpark II
Singapore 415956
Tel: (65) 6742-2088
Fax: (65) 6744-2088
enquiries@pageonegroup.com
www.pageonegroup.com

Distributed by:
Page One Publishing Private Limited
20 Kaki Bukit View
Kaki Bukit Techpark II
Singapore 415956
Tel: (65) 6742-2088
Fax: (65) 6744-2088

First published 2007 by Liaoning Science & Technology Press

Author   : Daniel Schulz
Editor   : Daniel Schulz
Jacket design : Beverly Chong

ISBN 978-981-245-607-6

Printed and bound by SNP Leefung Printers (Shenzhen) Co. Ltd.